Creative Ideas for
Wild Church

All accompanying colour pictures referred to in this book – and more! – are available for download at www.canterburypress.co.uk Please search for 'wild church'.

Creative Ideas for Wild Church

Mary Jackson
and
Juno Hollyhock

CANTERBURY
PRESS
Norwich

© Mary Jackson and Juno Hollyhock 2016

First published in 2016 by the Canterbury Press Norwich
Editorial office
3rd Floor, Invicta House
108–114 Golden Lane
London EC1Y 0TG, UK

Canterbury Press is an imprint of Hymns Ancient & Modern Ltd (a registered charity)
13A Hellesdon Park Road, Norwich,
Norfolk NR6 5DR, UK

www.canterburypress.co.uk

With the exception of page 24, which is from the English Standard Version,
Anglicized Edition © Collins, London, 2003, all Scripture quotations are from the
Holy Bible, New International Version. Copyright © 1973, 1978, 1984 by Biblica
(formally International Bible Society). Used by permission of Hodder & Stoughton
Ltd, a member of Hodder Headline Ltd.

British Library Cataloguing in Publication data

A catalogue record for this book is available
from the British Library

978 1 84825 881 5

Typeset by Regent Typesetting
Printed and bound in Great Britain by
Ashford Colour Press Ltd, Gosport, Hampshire

Contents

Foreword

'The earth is the Lord's, and everything in it, the world, and all who live in it', reads the lyric of Psalm 24, written by David, who I often think of as the Elvis of the Bible. Our God-given mandate to care for, protect and manage the wonderful and awe-inspiring creation, of which we are part, remains an all too often overlooked aspect of our Christian mission.

Wherever you dip into the Bible, it is clear that rather than calling for a two-way relationship between Creator and creatures, Scripture's real vision is for a triangular connection between the Creator, creatures and creation.

This 'green thread' runs throughout the Bible – from the creation stories of Genesis to the re-creation vision of a renewed heaven and earth in the Bible's last book, Revelation.

From the very outset, God inextricably linked humanity and creation. The planet was not simply created as a stage upon which we live our lives – we are part of creation: bonded to it and integrated into it seamlessly. 'For dust you are and to dust you will return', God explains in Genesis. Our responsibility is, and has always been – though we have been slow to see it – to love and respect the environment as well as its inhabitants.

In its very first book, following the famous statement that 'God saw all that he had made, and it was very good', humanity is solemnly charged with an ongoing role: the great responsibility and enormous joy of engaging with and caring for the natural environment.

And it's a mutually beneficial relationship. From the power of a crashing wave to the fragility of a butterfly – venturing into the fresh air inspires us to see life differently: to think of ourselves as part of, rather than apart from, our environment; to put our lives into perspective and discover new depths to our understanding of and relationship with the God of all creation.

Ranging from simple practical ideas on how to make the best use of your outside space to entire liturgies based on concepts rooted in the natural world, this book is intended to support all church leaders whether you want to take children's work out of doors, use the local park as a cathedral of praise, or create quiet and reflective spaces for prayer in a church yard.

I hope you will enjoy trying out some of these simple, easy to use ideas and helping your congregation to get to know nature a little better for what it is – God's wonderful creation.

Revd Steve Chalke
Founder of Oasis Global

For Lucy Scrase – may you always find God in the wild places.

Also for Small Saints at All Saints Church, Winchester,
for testing out many of the activities.

We thank friends and family for their patience, tolerance and love as
we have written this book, and for reading through our ideas.

About this book

This book is for every church: churches that usually meet inside but think that they might sometimes want to take their worship, their children's activities or their whole community outdoors, churches that already go outside occasionally but are looking for new ideas, and for churches that want to focus on the outdoors as a key part of what they do together.

Some churches might use this book for ideas for their children's or youth work to start with, but we hope they will find ideas that they can use with their wider church community too. Why should only the younger members of the congregation benefit from being outside, feeling the closeness to and wonder of God's creation?

Many churches are looking for new ways to engage with their wider community, and while some people find churches quite daunting and strange the outside environment can be one where more people may feel welcomed. It is a space that is generally less formal, less threatening and can be easily accessed and also 'escaped from' if someone feels uncomfortable.

Another area of work for churches is running a range of groups – so we have included activities that could be used with many of these. Some will work best with specific ages but many can be used in different ways with different groups, or with the whole church community. You will find that you can adapt them to make them your own.

We love being outside – and often feel that we get to know God better outside than we do in a church. We find outdoors a place of inspiration and creativity and being outside helps us to relate even better to the stories about Jesus, and those he told, many of which took place outside. Nature is essential to our lives and livelihoods in so many ways and we are nature's stewards, a role given to us by God. As such we believe that we have a responsibility to God to take nature seriously and think carefully about how we live our lives.

We wanted to write this book because we believe that in nature we find not only the reflection of our Creator but also the answer to so many questions in our lives. The space for reflection and contemplation that nature offers us is a soothing balm in an otherwise frenetic, electronically driven life. We believe that God gave us nature and its beauty as a form of healing – a chance to reconsider ourselves as a part of our environment, natural and precious and unique.

If by putting our thoughts down on paper we manage to persuade just one person to look up and out rather than down and in, to focus on the greatness around us and be grateful for it, and to bring some peace into their lives through the awe and wonder of the natural world, then that will be sufficient. In his grace we hope it may be so.

Introduction

Church is our chance to worship together, to meet with fellow Christians, to pray together and to prepare ourselves for the days ahead. For some, church is a Sunday morning family affair with interactive praise and lively songs, for others it is a quiet and reflective midweek service, a time to be still and to listen to God's word.

For many of us it is both of those things and many others besides.

We talk a lot in church about God's creation, about his wonderful world and our part in it.

We often reflect upon biblical passages that evoke nature and the outdoors. Verses 1 and 2 of Psalm 23 show us how important the role of nature is in God's plan for us.

The Lord is my shepherd, I lack nothing.
He makes me lie down in green pastures, he leads me beside quiet waters.

Yet so often our worship and contemplation takes place within four walls, away from sunlight and the beauty of the world.

If you want to try something different, if you want to make worship and reflection a multi-sensory experience, and if you want to dwell upon the awesome splendour of God in the perfection of the smallest detail of nature, then this book is for you.

About Juno and Mary

Juno

While working as Youth and Children's Ministry Advisor for the Anglican Diocese of Portsmouth, Juno contributed services to the Church House Publishing series 'Worship Through the Christian Year – All Age Resources for the Three Year Lectionary'.

During her time with the Church of England Juno supported the work of the child protection teams in parishes and was instrumental in helping to coordinate the first ever Church of England Conference on Child Protection.

Before becoming Executive Director for Learning through Landscapes Juno worked for Steve Chalke, minister, evangelist and founder of Oasis UK, supporting the development of the Oasis family of academies. She remains chair of the academy council for one of Steve's early secondary academies.

Throughout her life Juno has been convinced of the role of nature and the natural environment in a healthy, balanced life. She feels that engagement with nature reminds us that we are but a small part of God's wonderful creation, and that can help bring peace and perspective in a world where problems can swiftly get out of hand.

Juno is a keen walker and gardener and loves nothing better than lying on a warm grassy hill making shapes out of clouds.

Mary

For the last 20 years Mary has helped adults and children get outside more – something she has done herself as a child and also an adult. Much of this work has been with schools, while currently she is a member of a church that is not scared to go outdoors occasionally. At All Saints Church, Winchester she helps to run the children's activities – a great test bed for the ideas within this book. This experience, combined with working with a church who have an outside space to develop, got her wondering if other churches might like to get outside more and how she could bring her knowledge to help them do this. She has written a number of resources to help schools get outside and regularly runs training to help teachers and parents take children and young people outdoors.

Mary was the main author for a book on developing primary school grounds published by Learning through Landscapes (*Learn and Play Out*), as well as writing numerous resources for teachers on taking lessons outside. She is an experienced trainer, teaching teachers how to teach outside and landscape architects how to design great school grounds. She is the co-founder and a member of the Leadership Council of the International School Grounds Alliance, which has over 500 members in 20 countries across the globe.

Recently she has been working with a number of churches to help them plan their own developments outside – whether making changes to their grounds or looking at how their communities can take their activities and services out more.

Getting started

Bringing the outside in

Look and listen

If you are not yet quite ready to take church outside, or you want to better reflect God's wonderful kingdom inside your worship space, then there are some simple things you can do.

Often in our services we sit inside and focus on a screen, on our singing or on the words of the leader in front of us. By drawing the congregation's attention to the outside through words and song we can build an awareness of nature going about its business as we worship together.

Invite people to spend a moment in silence and identify what they can hear of the outside. Is there a window that you can open? What can they hear – is there birdsong perhaps, or can they hear the wind? Is it raining heavily?

Just the act of listening helps to bring nature into our hearts.

Invite people to look at the shafts of sunlight as they fall through the windows; perhaps turn the lights off in the church if the weather is dull and reflect on the light and dark of nature. Evening services held partly in candlelight remind us of the natural patterns of the seasons that God created.

Nature is everywhere

Even in the most urban settings nature will creep in – in the dandelions between the paving stones, the grass on the verge, the rosebay willow herb on the building site and the tiny creatures that go about their business in the air and under the ground.

And we, of course, are also an intrinsic part of nature ourselves.

Be seasonal

Foliage hanging

If you are lucky enough to live in an area where it is possible to gather natural materials, think about how you might collect local seasonal items such as leaves, branches, seed heads, flowers and fruits. These can be displayed inside your church building, giving a sense of the passing of the seasons with the change of the display. This is a fun activity for Junior Church, and different age groups can take it in turns with the different seasons. The displays don't need to be perfect: old fallen branches hung with berries or piles of misshapen fruit are valuable reflections of nature. (See colour photo of foliage hanging in winter display on the website.)

Ivy draped around noticeboards is long-lasting and can have a great effect.

Be bold

Be brave and bold with nature – why not have a log pile indoors or strew the aisle with fallen autumn leaves, or arrange choir seating on hay bales – yes, there will be some mess but the impact of nature meeting the worshipping space can be very powerful, especially for people who perhaps don't have access to gardens at home.

The children will certainly find this fun and engaging!

Leave the piles in place for a few weeks and arrange a big church cleaning hour one morning after the service – cleaning together is a positive activity and everyone will have enjoyed the novelty of what went before.

Winter display

Plant nature

If you would welcome a more permanent piece of nature in your space then consider investing in some large indoor planters. These can be planted up with flowers and shrubs that suit your light and shade – maybe some beautiful flowers for a sunny spot by a window, or you could place ferns in the darker areas.

Introducing plants and foliage will soften the edges and create texture and points of focus and reflection. Try and make sure that something is growing all year round, and remember to agree a watering rota!

Picture this

Images are very powerful, and just refreshing what is on the walls of your church and church hall can help to bring the outside in.

Use strong images of landscapes – encourage people to get out and about with their cameras. Make sure that you include local images too; these may be very rural or very urban, but they can all include visions of nature (remember those dandelions!). Perhaps consider going on a whole church walk, for instance on Good Friday, and take some images of everyone together enjoying the benefits of the natural world.

You might like to get some images from overseas – images that remind us of our brothers and sisters in other parts of the world. This can help us as we focus on praying for our world and also reminds us that nature's beauty has many manifestations.

Use images to support talks, and consider how the pictures that you use on PowerPoint and projections can help bring nature inside.

You could even consider how images used to decorate vestments, kneelers, tapestries and cloths might be designed to reflect nature and the outside world.

Get techy

Those who have the inclination could use technology to help bring the outside in. A webcam installed in a bird box can bring joy and delight to a Sunday school or Junior Church session as we watch the miracle of little families living and growing on our church grounds. There are so many lessons to be learned from the way in which baby birds depend on their parents, who work so hard to bring them food, and the way in which God cares for all creatures.

Nature is essential

Getting closer to nature is good for all of us but we don't all have the chance to get out and about as much as we would like.

Some of us maybe don't even think about our relationship with nature because we are too busy, because we live away from a natural environment or because we weren't brought up to value the natural world.

By introducing nature into our worshipping life we can follow the seasons and identify with a sense of time, we can recognize our part in nature, we can address and discuss issues of stewardship of our God-given world and we can explore the beauty and the miracles that happen around us every single day.

Putting together your outdoor church kit

Sometimes you will have planned in advance to go outside; at other times you might just think it is a lovely day and it's a shame to be indoors. Sometimes you can just go outside and may not need to take anything special with you; however, if you want to take activities or services outside on a regular basis it is a good idea to create a kit that you keep ready so that you can head outdoors whenever you want to.

Every church's kit will be slightly different depending on what you have outside, what storage you have available and what types of activity you want to do outdoors. The list we have put together is a starting point. You may find that it includes some things you never use, while other things are not listed that you will find make your outdoor sessions work for you.

You will need to think about where you are going to store your kit. Consider outdoor storage. This will need to be waterproof and able to be secured but will make it easier for you to use your outside space more often.

Create a list of your kit or take a photograph of what it contains so that everyone knows that they have put it all back when they have finished. Provide a system of reporting breakages or losses so that you can update your kit when necessary.

Essentials

- A first aid kit (and ensure that someone knows how to use it).
  - Make sure you add in wipes and creams to treat stings, bites and scratches as these might not be in your indoor first aid kit.
- Something to sit on.
  - Even if you have outdoor seating, unless it is covered there will be times when you need something to sit on.

- Movable seating can include rugs and blankets, tarpaulins, outdoor bean bags or cushions. You can also put newspaper into carrier bags to put on the ground, or a damp seat, to sit on.
- Something for shade or shelter if you don't have a permanent structure or suitable trees to sit under.
  - Umbrellas, sheets and tarpaulins that you can drape over structures or over ropes hung between trees or buildings, and something to tie them with, e.g. ropes, bungie cords, clothes pegs.
- A Bible or two you don't mind going outside (children's versions as well as adult ones will be useful).
- Clipboards, paper and pencils and crayons so that you can write things down or draw whenever you want to.
- Wet wipes are useful to clean hands when you have been handling things outside.
- A whistle to call everyone back together.

Other useful bits and pieces

- Bags and other containers such as boxes and tins.
- Torches.
- Chalk – both white and coloured.
- Long strips of cloth about 5–10cm wide (tear up an old sheet or duvet) – these are useful to mark out spaces and patterns. They can also be useful to tie things up with instead of rope.
- Wallpaper lining paper – a cheap way to have a ready supply of paper for everyone to use.

Useful extras for specific activities

- Fire outside:
  - A barbecue, fire wok or other similar container for your fire (if you don't have anything permanent).
  - A bucket for water (and an outdoor tap).
  - Fire steels and cotton wool or matches and paper in an air-tight tin.
  - Small sticks or other kindling (always having something dry will help you get your fire going).
  - Gauntlets, oven gloves or other protection to help you handle hot items.

- – A simple cooking kit such as pots and pans, large spoons and fish slices.
- – A container for drinking water.
- – An outdoor kettle.
- – Long, sturdy sticks for tending the fire.

- Art outside:
  - – A selection of paint brushes including decorators' brushes.
  - – Water pots for cleaning brushes in.
  - – Extra wallpaper lining paper.
  - – Other paper for drawing or painting on.
  - – A mixture of pencils, crayons and felt-tip pens, paints, etc.
  - – Pots to mix paints in.
  - – Glue.
  - – Scissors.
  - – Secateurs for cutting foliage that you could use to create your art.

If you are going outside a lot, especially with children, you may even want to think about investing in some all-weather gear. This might include wellington boots, waterproof ponchos, hats and gloves.

What happens if it rains and other problems?

Dealing with the weather

It has been said many a time that there is no such thing as bad weather, just inappropriate clothing. This is fine if you are working with a youth group or doing an activity that you expect to wear particular clothes for, but not so easy when you are planning a service or bringing together people who are not used to being outside for church. So it is particularly important that you take the weather into account in your planning.

- First – check the weather forecast. These days the forecast is pretty accurate for at least five days so you can have a good idea of what you need to prepare for and, if necessary, add weather protection or even bring things inside.
- Be sensible – sometimes you will need to come indoors. This might be because it is too wet, or too hot, and you have nowhere suitable to shelter or surfaces are too slippery for what you want to do. If you are finding it hard to decide whether or not it is safe, undertake a risk-benefit assessment before you start (see 'What about health and safety?') and this will help you make the right choices. If necessary be pragmatic and bring things indoors for safety reasons but don't make this an excuse just because it is a bit wet or chilly.

Remember that you want to keep people enthusiastic about taking activities and services outside so there is no point in going outside for the sake of it and putting people off because of the weather. Children are likely to be more accommodating than adults as far as this is concerned so you might stay outside with children in conditions that you would come in for with the wider church community.

Shade and shelter

Check out where you are doing your activity before you start. Is there somewhere to shelter from the rain or the sun? Where will shade fall when you are going to be outside? Can you create temporary shade and shelter or even plan something more permanent for the future? Some ways of creating shade and shelter include:

- Shade sails – we have used actual sails for this, using ropes and bungie cords to attach them to the building, fences and trees. You can just as easily use sheets or blankets. Just think about where the shade is going to be not only when you put the sails up but throughout the time you are outside. You can buy manufactured shade sails if you want something more permanent.
- Trees provide ready-made shade or shelter on sunny or even drizzly days. Planning for the long term, you may want to consider planting something for the future.
- Pergolas or other more permanent structures – these may be difficult to erect because of planning permission and other people's use of the site. However, if you have a nursery or playgroup on your site they may also find this type of structure useful so think about creating something alongside your church hall or parish rooms. In time, you could grow climbers over this type of structure which will provide more shade in the summer while allowing light through in the winter.
- In the summer large umbrellas can be a quick and easy way of creating shade.
- Other temporary shade and shelter can be made using tarpaulins or sheets – they can also bring colour to your space.
- Children will love making dens outside and these instantly provide them with some shade.

Music and sound

- If you want to hold a service outside you need to consider how to take the music and sound systems outside – especially if you are using a loop system.
- You may have a music group, in which case it could be relatively straightforward to have music outside, but if you usually use an organ you will need to experiment as to how to ensure that this can be heard outdoors, or try something else for a change.
- A loop system may be hard to adapt. Talk with those who use it and work out the best way for them to ensure that they do not lose out when you go outside. This may mean that they need to have seats where they can see those speaking, that there are subtitles, pictures or handouts to support what is being said or sung, or you may need to provide an interpreter for those who sign.

Seating

- Many churches use seats instead of pews so going outside may simply be a case of moving the seats to the outdoors.
- Children often find it hard to see and hear what is going on, so having picnic rugs at the front of your seating can be a great way for them to feel really involved. You could ask families to bring rugs along for your event or service and they can then sit together in a more informal setting.
- Other forms of temporary seating can include straw bales, waterproof bean bags or large cushions, tarpaulins, newspapers inside carrier bags or carpet tiles.
- If you are creating a permanent space outside then you will need to consider the type and layout of seating that will be most appropriate for what you will be using it for.

At the end of this book there is a separate section on planning your outside space, so if you are thinking about changing your space do take a look there for ideas on how to plan this.

Permanent seating

What about health and safety?

Health and safety is really important and must not be ignored; however, don't let it be the reason you don't go outside unless it is really not sensible for you to venture out.

For many of the activities in this book you will not need to undertake specific risk assessments or risk-benefit assessments as they do not have any higher levels of hazard or risk than your usual activities inside. However, it is a good idea to undertake a general risk-benefit assessment of your grounds, so that you have identified any general risks and hazards that will be faced every time you go outdoors. Make sure that this assessment is easily accessible to all, and if there are any issues these should be made known to anyone going outside. You can then take most activities outside without doing an individual risk-benefit assessment each time you go.

Health and safety is mainly about common sense but make sure you don't just leave this to 'someone else'. Someone should have specific responsibility for health and safety for outdoors or for a particular activity so that you consider all the safety precautions that might need to be taken.

If there are any doubts about the safety of an activity, carry out a specific risk-benefit assessment (see below). Start by looking at the benefits of your activity, then consider the various hazards you might come across when undertaking the particular activity, and the chances of these happening – the risk.

In the case of using fire, benefits might include a group working together outside, eating together, and sharing an exciting experience; hazards would include burns from the fire or other hot objects. What is the chance, or risk, of this happening? Consider what you need to do to make sure that this is unlikely to happen.

There will always be some risks when working outdoors, and the benefits of carrying out an activity need to be balanced with the chance of the hazard occurring. A risk-benefit assessment will make sure that you are as safe as necessary and help you to decide whether an activity is suitable in a given situation. The key is to be as safe as you need to be rather than being as safe as possible. If you are as safe as possible you will never go outside, or do anything, at all.

Risk-benefit assessment

Many people will be familiar with a risk assessment but not necessarily a risk-benefit assessment. You start by looking at the benefits of the activity, then you look at the potential hazards – things that could cause problems, and the chance of them happening – the risks. You then look at the scale of the hazard and its risk combined. The larger the hazard the lower the risk level needs to be for you to consider it is safe enough to take place. So small injuries such as a minor burn might be likely but acceptable, while a serious burn is only acceptable, if it is very unlikely to happen. If the overall rating is high then you will either not undertake the activity or make changes to lower the risk level.

If you find the risks of something happening are too high when balanced against the benefits of the activity you can do one of two things: either not undertake the activity, or see if you can reduce the risk to an acceptable level. It is likely that all low-risk activities can be carried out and high-risk activities will be avoided. It is those at the medium level that you need to balance risks against benefits most carefully.

Example of part of a risk-benefit assessment table.

Activity	Benefit of activity	Possible hazards	Level of risk before action	Action to reduce risk level	Overall rating – low, medium or high	Benefit outweighs the risk
Graveyard treasure hunt	To discover more about the history of the church and community.	Trip hazards, overhead branches, etc., potentially slippery paths, uneven ground, poisonous plants, strangers.	Medium	Remind participants of hazards, adults supervising children and watching out for strangers, first aider available.	Low	Yes

You will also need to make changes to your assessment as the activity happens; this is known as a dynamic risk assessment. What this means is that you need to keep your eye out for any unexpected events and consider if the risk has as a result become too high for the activity to still be safe. Things will happen that you don't expect but few will stop you from continuing what you are doing.

Generally you will find that there are no major risks to being outside in your church grounds and that the benefits will far outweigh these. Make sure you don't use health and safety as an excuse not to get outdoors.

Specific information for working with fire

- Health and safety is really important when using fire.
- Do not leave a fire unattended, however large or small, for any length of time, unless you are sure it is completely extinguished.
- You should never start a fire if you don't have a means for putting it out, so make sure you have a water supply and sand nearby.
- Always carry out a simple risk-benefit assessment (see above) before using fire. If you are using a barbecue, fire wok or camp fire make sure it is well out of the way of general activity so that no one accidentally trips over it, especially children. It is a good idea to mark out a circle a few yards around the fire. This is where most people will sit or stand, well out of the reach of the fire itself. Only those tending or cooking over the fire should approach the fire. If anyone needs to move around they should step outside the circle to move before returning inside the ring when they have reached their destination.
- Anyone tending a low fire should kneel down on at least one knee so that they have a stable base in case anyone should bump into them from behind. Those in wheelchairs or seated on a regular chair will already have a good solid base to tend the fire from. This same position should be used when cooking over the fire. Even very young children can take part in activity around a fire if they are told how to behave and supervised carefully by adults.
- Have a first aid kit with you and make sure someone knows how to use it.
- Make sure that you have water ready nearby for putting out the fire if necessary or to cool minor burns (running water is always better for this). Minor burns should be treated by holding under running cold water for ten minutes; anything more serious requires medical attention. You should only ever cover burns with a sterile dressing or kitchen film.
- When you leave the fire make sure it is fully extinguished so that there is no risk of it relighting.

- If you are cooking food and eating it, make sure you also have access to water for cleaning your hands. A first bucket of water can be used for getting the worst of any dirt off and a second one used for rinsing hands.

Other health and safety issues to consider when going outside

- **Trip hazards** – make sure that routes are clear, especially if people are moving fast and not necessarily looking where they are going. Some trip hazards will always be there, so everyone needs to be aware that outside is not as controlled as inside and to watch where they are going.
- **Unexpected objects at head height** – there will be more of these outside than indoors. Remember that people are different heights so look above and below your own eye level when reviewing a site.
- **Slippery surfaces** – check surfaces out, especially on damp days, and decide if any particular areas or routes need to be avoided, cleared or made safe.
- **Traffic** – this is particularly important when you are working with children. Make sure that exits to roads from where you are working are secure or well supervised. When you are going somewhere different, or crossing roads, you need to have enough adults to supervise, especially when you are with young children.
- **Stranger danger** – you may be using places that are open to the public, so be aware of any people approaching your group that you do not know, especially if you are working with children or vulnerable adults.
- **Animals** – again in public spaces there may be animals in the area that you may not be able to control. Be aware that you need to be able to protect the members of your group.
- **Poisonous and irritant plants** – if you are accompanying very young children look out for poisonous plants that might seem attractive to touch or to eat. Other plants may just be an irritant, such as stinging nettles, but might cause a few tears along the way.
- **Allergies** – some people have allergies that can affect them badly at certain times of year, such as hay fever, and this may well stop them from enjoying being outdoors. Check that children have any medication with them if needed; if they are very young, you should know how and when it needs to be administered. You also need to be aware of any food allergies if you are eating outside.

Specific things to remember if you are travelling off-site

- If you are taking children and young people off-site outside their usual session time then you should ensure you have permission from parents and carers.
- If you are taking any groups off-site for any length of time, participants, parents and carers need to be given the following information:
  - Where you are going.
  - What the purpose is of your trip.
  - Transport details.
  - Times for departure and return.
  - What they need to take with them – what to wear, any food required, equipment, etc.
  - Your contact details.
- You will need from them:
  - A list of any allergies and intolerances – and not just for foods but for stings, bites and plants.
  - Any medical information about children and young people including doctors' contact details.
  - A list of parents' or carers' contact details – especially when taking children, young people or vulnerable adults off-site.
- Make sure you undertake a risk-benefit assessment for your trip – this should be signed by all the adults helping to organize and run your visit.
- Make sure you have appropriate numbers of adults to supervise the children and young people who are on the trip.

Working with children

Generally the rules for working with children outside are the same as those for being inside. Adult to child ratio recommendations are the same for outside as for inside; however, you may feel more confident if you have a higher number of adults when using an unfamiliar site or somewhere that has open access. You will also need to ensure that your children's workers have undertaken the appropriate disclosure and barring services (DBS) checks.

The NSPCC recommends the following ratios when supervising children:

Aged 0–2 years: 1 adult to 3 children
Aged 2–3 years: 1 adult to 4 children
Aged 4–8 years: 1 adult to 6 children

Aged 9–12 years: 1 adult to 8 children
Aged 13–18 years: 1 adult to 10 children

For a mixed group it is recommended that supervising staff should include male and female members.

When you go outside make sure that children understand what you expect of them. For example, you are not just going outside to play; they need to know where the boundaries are, and that they should return to you on your signal – a whistle is ideal for this. It is a good idea to try this out the first time you go outside to check that they understand that they should return to you when you blow your whistle.

Insurance

You need to check that your insurance covers you for the variety of activities you want to do outside and for all the people who will be getting involved. If you are at all uncertain about whether you are covered, get in touch with your broker.

If you are planning to make physical changes to the outside space using members of your church community as workers, make sure that you are covered both for undertaking the tasks yourselves and then for using these facilities once they have been completed.

How do we include everyone?

Accessibility and inclusivity

Whatever you are doing, consider how accessible the activities are for everyone who may get involved. Remember that while not everything you do can be ideal for everyone, you should still make sure that you don't exclude anyone who wants to take part.

Consider the accessibility of the site as a starting point: routes, pathways, seating, sound and vision. Can everybody access what you are doing outside? Can those who use the loop system in church still understand what is going on outdoors? If someone uses Braille versions of songs or hymns, can they also use them outside? If you have a sign interpreter can they be easily seen by those who are accessing the service or activity in this way?

If you are using other types of interpreter, make sure that they can be easily heard. Working in small groups can make communication easier for those with hearing or language issues. External noises can interfere with hearing, so make sure that what is going on is audible to everyone, especially for those who have hearing loss, who need to be positioned near to speakers so that the sound does not dissipate before it reaches them.

Avoid participants having to look into the sun or be upwind of those speaking. Let the leaders look into the sun if necessary and ensure that their voices travel with the wind not against it. Look at the sight lines between those leading and those observing; make sure that nothing obstructs the view of the congregation during a service, for example.

Do people from different cultural groups within the church feel comfortable with what you are doing? It may well be that you want to share one group's enthusiasms or ideas with another group, but it is important that no one attending is offended by this. Is the imagery being used inclusive of the different groups within your church and wider community?

Can people with different levels of literacy be fully involved with the activity? Will anyone feel left out in this way by anything you are doing?

If you have members of your community with dementia then creating outside spaces that they can engage with can be very valuable. Information about dementia-friendly space can be obtained from Step Change Design: www.stepchange-design.co.uk; Thrive: www.thrive.org.uk; Sensory Trust: www.sensorytrust.org.uk; and Alzheimer's Society: www.alzheimers.org.uk. Be aware that some people struggle with open spaces and are happier when there is a hedge or a fence as a boundary.

Consider the physical access to the site: the pathways, gateways and issues such as uneven ground. Make sure any routes to unsecured areas are carefully observed, if you cannot block them off completely, so that children do not go into them unsupervised. Think about the need for proper seats rather than just bench seats, which are often used outside but are not comfortable for everyone. Make sure that there are seating options available with backs, and also arms for people to push up on when they are getting up.

Don't forget that you may be outside in a space that other people and animals have access to. Remember to provide hand-washing facilities for people if they will be handling things outdoors, especially if they are then going to eat.

Children and adults use outdoor spaces in different ways. You might need to work at getting adults used to being outdoors, or separate children from the wider group. Providing extra supervision for the younger members of your community will help the parents relax.

Think about the people in your community who don't usually come to church. Can activities outside be events that they might feel comfortable to come to?

Is what you plan to do appropriate for the age of those taking part? Will all the children have something appropriate to do, for example? Are there activities suitable for older people as well as younger ones?

Above all, think through how your service or activity is going to work. As long as you have planned well how the different groups and individuals within your community can engage with what you are doing, you will succeed.

Autumn

Creating from creation

In this activity children create a large-scale outdoor picture of the story of creation, made from materials they find outdoors.

Focus: The beauty and variety of creation and the creation story.
Type of activity: A Sunday school activity or part of a family activity day.
Age range: 6 to 16 years, or the whole church family.
Resources:

- Bags or baskets to collect natural resources in and an outside area in which to find your materials. You may want to collect some beforehand, depending on where you are located and the time available.
- The type of items to collect are: pebbles, sticks and branches, leaves, feathers, flowers, seeds and fruits.
- A space to create your artwork – ideally outside.

Aim

The aim of the session is for participants to focus on the beauty and wonder of God's creation by engaging with it and creating an artwork in celebration.

Structure

Reading
Talking with the children
The outdoors bit
   Collecting your materials
   Making your picture
   Bringing it all together
   Prayer

Reading

Start by gathering everyone together, ideally outside, and read the story of the creation from Genesis, chapter 1 and 2.1–3 (use a child-friendly version).

Talking with the children (and whole group)

The reading in Genesis tells us the story of creation, broken down into the specific elements being created on different days. As you go through, highlight what was created on each day and that it was written this way to help us remember that God made the world.

Day 1 – Light and dark – night and day.
Day 2 – Separating the waters – sky, land and seas.
Day 3 – The land produces vegetation.
Day 4 – The sun and the moon – creation of the seasons.
Day 5 – Creatures of the land and the seas.
Day 6 – Human beings.
Day 7 – Rest.

God created the world but we are responsible for looking after it. Talk to the children about what you need in order to be able to do this. Questions to ask might include:

• Have you ever grown anything yourself?
• If so, what did you have to do to look after it? Plant it in soil, water it, feed it, keep it in the sunlight.
• Do any of you own pets? What do you have to do to care for them? Feed them, give them water, take them for a walk, provide them with somewhere to sleep, take them to the vet if they get ill or injured.
• What happens if you don't look after things properly? Plants won't grow well; pets may die.
• While many plants and animals around us appear to get on OK without us the truth is that we actually do have an impact on other living things by what we do every day. If we leave litter, animals might eat it or get trapped in it; both these things may do them harm. If we pollute the world, we can make plants and animals ill; we can contribute to climate change, which means that some plants and animals find it hard to live where they are meant to. By planting trees and growing other plants or making a pond we can create habitats that

can help more animals to live there. But we still need to look after all these things to make sure they are healthy and can survive.

- What happens in your garden in the summer? The soil gets very dry, and the grass may go brown. You may need to water the garden for everything to grow well.
- All these plants and animals are part of God's creation. It is therefore important that we look after them and are thankful for everything that lives around us.

We are going to create a picture (or series of pictures) of the story of creation using bits and pieces we find outside. This is going to be a celebration of God's creation and we are going to make it outside so that lots of people can see it and also be thankful for the natural world.

The outdoors bit

Collecting your materials

Take the children to a place where they can collect a variety of natural materials, e.g. sticks and stones, leaves and flowers, pebbles and seeds. You will need a selection of bags or baskets for the children to collect their items in.

This activity is best done if children collect their own special items but you can also offer them a supply of items to work with such as flowers, stones, twigs and leaves (which are particularly lovely to use in the autumn). A sandy beach is another good space as you have a 'canvas' in the sand, and can collect pebbles, seaweed, shells and driftwood to make your pictures with.

Making your picture

Bring the items back to your church grounds, or whatever location you are using, to create your picture; if possible, find a space where people passing by can see what you are doing and the final result.

In this space you are going to create a picture, or series of pictures, of creation. Build it in the same order as the creation story in Genesis, adding the features for each day described to the picture.

Day 1 – Light and dark – night and day. Make the outline frame of your picture, using sticks or pebbles or drawing the frame in the sand (if on a beach) or with chalk (if on asphalt).

Day 2 – Separating the waters – sky, land and seas. Make the main landscape elements – hills, seas and the sky. You could do this with sticks, pebbles, leaves, etc.

Day 3 – The land produces vegetation – make trees, shrubs and flowers out of natural materials.

Day 4 – The sun and the moon – the creation of the seasons. Make a shining sun to one side of your picture (you may wish to make a moon and star for the other side).

Day 5 – Creatures of the land and the seas – make a collection of different creatures. (See colour photos on the website for the following examples: A hedgehog made from a teasel and berries. A rabbit made from a pine cone and seeds. A fish made on a beach from seaweed and shells.)

Day 6 – Human beings – you now need to make some people to live in your creation, and add these to your picture too.

Day 7 – Rest – your picture is finished. Add a title to your picture.

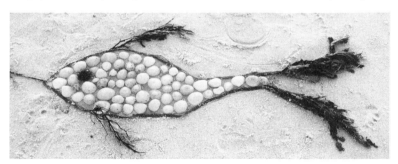

A fish on a beach made from seaweed and shells

A hedgehog made from a teasel and berries

A rabbit made from a pine cone and seeds

Be as creative as you can with your design – the children will have lots of ideas. If you are a bit stuck, here are some suggestions to get you going. (See colour photo of an example of a picture at day 5 on the website.)

- Sticks and leaves become trees.
- Feathers become birds.
- Sweet chestnut nut cases become hedgehogs with berries as eyes.
- A pine cone with a sycamore helicopter becomes a rabbit.
- On the beach you could create an underwater scene using seaweed, pebbles and shells.

A picture entitled 'Creation'

Children of all ages will enjoy working together, as will adults, everyone adding their own ideas to the picture. The youngest children can work with an adult to help them create features that fit in.

Leave the picture outside for as long as you can, so that other people can see what you have created.

Bringing it all together

At the end gather the children around their picture. Take a photograph of your work so that you can display inside what you have achieved, and remember it after it has been dismantled. Ask the children to remind you of the order they did everything, which is the order of the days of creation in the Bible. They are much more likely to remember this than if you had only read the story.

Prayer

When you have completed your artwork collect together the natural materials you have left over. Everyone should choose one of the items from this selection.

Ask them to either say or think of a prayer thanking God for his wonderful creation as they bring their selected item to a gathering point and create a prayerful pile of natural wonders. You could even wrap them up as a gift to God, offering what he has given us back to him. Make sure that any material you use for wrapping the things up is biodegradable, reusable or recyclable, if at all possible, and that it won't harm any animals if it is left outside.

It can be useful to give children suggestions as to how to begin their prayer. Here are some starting points you might use:

- Thank you, God, for making the world. I especially thank you for . . .
- The world around us is beautiful. Thank you, Lord, for giving us a beautiful world to live in. I want to thank you for . . .
- Thank you, Lord, for everything in the world, the big things and the small, the bright coloured things and those that might look a bit dull. Help us to look after the world around us and help me to look after . . .

When you are ready, return your materials to the natural world – or let your beach picture be washed away. Any man-made materials should be returned, recycled or thrown away responsibly.

The festival of Sukkot

In this activity members of the whole church community build simple shelters as part of learning about the Feast of the Tabernacles. Included is a description of the different ways these can then be used: for meeting places, spaces for quiet and for prayer or for play dens for children.

Focus: Learning about the Jewish festival of the Feast of the Tabernacles (Leviticus 23.33–44) and creating shelters.
Type of activity: To be part of a family awayday or weekend away.
Age range: The whole church community.
Resources:

- Materials to make shelters with – branches for the roofs (branches can be real or home-made), and perhaps sheets, tarpaulins or canvas for the walls.
- You might want to use some form of structure to hold up your shelter – this might be poles, broom handles, clothes airers.
- Clothes pegs, bungie cords, rope, strips of cloth and string are always useful.
- Rugs, cushions, bean bags or carpet tiles are good for sitting on.
- You can also add decorations to your shelter – pictures, lanterns, flowers, crops, etc.

Aim

To bring the whole church community together in an activity that encourages them to look at the story of the Jews while creating shelters that can be used later on in a time outside together.

Structure

About the festival
Reading

The outdoors bit
  Making the shelters or Sukkah
  Using the shelters

About the festival

Sukkot is celebrated in the autumn but not on the same date each year. You can find the date by going to www.timeanddate.com/holidays/uk/sukkot. It is observed during the week starting on the 15th day of Tishri (or Tishrei), which is the first month of the year in the Jewish calendar (this usually occurs in September or October).

The festival of Sukkot commemorates the years the Jews spent in the desert as they made their way to the promised land. Making open-air shelters is a way to remember this time, when the Jewish people lived in temporary shelters for 40 years.

Reading

Leviticus 23.33–44
The Festival of Tabernacles
The Lord said to Moses, 'Say to the Israelites: "On the fifteenth day of the seventh month the Lord's Festival of Tabernacles begins, and it lasts for seven days. The first day is a sacred assembly; do not do any of your ordinary work. For seven days present food offerings to the Lord, and on the eighth day hold a sacred assembly and present a food offering to the Lord. It is the closing special assembly; do not do any of your ordinary work.

('"These are the Lord's appointed festivals, which you are to proclaim as sacred assemblies for bringing food offerings to the Lord – the burnt offerings and grain offerings, sacrifices and drink offerings required for each day. These offerings are in addition to those for the Lord's Sabbaths and in addition to your gifts and whatever you have vowed and all the freewill offerings you give to the Lord.)

'"So beginning with the fifteenth day of the seventh month, after you have gathered the crops of the land, celebrate the festival to the Lord for seven days; the first day is a day of sabbath rest, and the eighth day also is a day of sabbath rest. On the first day you are to take branches from luxuriant trees – from palms, willows and other leafy trees – and rejoice before the Lord your God for seven days. Celebrate this as a festival to the Lord for seven days each year. This is to be a lasting ordinance for the generations to come; celebrate it in the seventh month. Live in temporary shelters for seven days: all native-born Israelites are to live in such shelters so that your descendants will know that I made the Israelites live in temporary shelters when I brought them out of Egypt. I am the Lord your God.'"

So Moses announced to the Israelites the appointed festivals of the Lord.

This passage describes God explaining to Moses what should happen during the festival:

- It starts on the fifteenth day of the seventh month after the harvest has been gathered.
- It lasts for seven days.
- The first day is a sacred assembly and a day of rest.
- The temporary shelters are made and for seven days food offerings are presented.
- On the eighth day a sacred assembly is held and it is also a day of rest.

John 7.2 also mentions the Festival of the Tabernacles.

The outdoors bit

Making the shelters or Sukkah

The key features of your Sukkah should be as follows:

- You should locate your Sukkah in the open – not under the branches of a tree or under the shelter of another structure.
- The roof of your shelter should not be solid – the idea is that you can see the sky through the roof. It should be covered with vegetation that has not been used for any other purposes, e.g. branches.
- Each wall should be at least 1 metre in height. The inside dimensions should be at least 60cm by 60cm but there is no maximum length or breadth.
- A Sukkah would not be used for more than one year; a new one should be made each year.

These are two examples of ways of making a Sukkah, although you can make yours any way you want:

1. Use clothes horses to form a free-standing structure. This will make quite a low shelter, so probably suitable for children to use. However, you could use similar elements and make one big enough to fit several people in. (See illustration.)

A Sukkah

- The clothes horses form a frame for your Sukkah – use string, rope or garden wire coated with plastic to secure them together.
- Across the top lay bamboo canes. Attach these at either end with string. These will make the structure sturdy and should be easy to attach as the shelter will be quite low in height.
- Make the walls of your shelter with blankets or sheets – attaching these with clothes pegs works well.
- Strew foliage over the top of your shelter, making sure you can still see the sky through the roof.

2. Use existing structures to create a shelter.

- Using netting for your roof, attach this to any solid structure you have available. This might be the outside of a building, in which case this will make one of your walls, or a tree. Use bungie cords or rope to make your attachments.
- Spread foliage over your roof, remembering that you should be able to see the sky through it.
- Sheets, tarpaulins or blankets can be added to make further walls.

Inside the structure you can have a table or rug to lay your feast out on and add seats, cushions, bean bags or rugs to sit on.

Hang decorations from the roof or walls and add flowers, crops or pictures drawn by the children.

Throughout the festival people eat meals in the shelters. Some people might want to camp out in them too, in which case you will need to add a weatherproof covering.

Using the shelters

Once you have the shelters built they can be used in various different ways throughout your time together as a church family.

Traditionally a Sukkah is used for eight days, during which time it becomes an 'official home'. However, this can mean just eating meals in your hut. Jews will also undertake in their Sukkah other activities normally carried out in a house, such as reading a book or talking with a friend.

Church groups are unlikely to follow this as strictly, so you could use your shelter in other ways. Whatever you choose to do, make sure that you are respectful of their traditional use and their relevance to the Jewish community. Some suggestions are:

- For small groups to meet in for quiet activities such as Bible study or prayer or for planning further activities, i.e. it can be a meeting space.
- For people to retire to on their own for peace and quiet, away from the hustle and bustle of other activities.
- To shelter in if it is wet (although the holes in the roof won't stop much rain!), or sunny.
- To gather in to share a meal.
- You can extend the main structure over your time together, or add Bible verses, images or colour to your shelter, maybe hanging items like decorations from the roof or pinned to the walls.
- For camping out, in which case you will need a good waterproof cover, both below and above you, whether or not rain is forecast.

Concepts of perfection

SERVICE

Focus: To understand how our drive to achieve what we see as 'perfect' can get in the way of our relationship with God. By recognizing the value in all things, including ourselves, and recognizing our service as unique to God, we can enter into a deeper sense of what it is to be his child.

We want people to go away from the service reflecting on how they view the world and the people in it and feeling a greater sense of peace in their relationship with God.

Resources:
- Somewhere outside where it is possible to gather fallen leaves.
- Bucket of warm water and a towel.

WE GATHER FOR WORSHIP

Welcome, everyone, to our outdoor service.

Today we are going to be thinking about what it means to be perfect. What our understanding of perfect is – and challenging ourselves to consider if our perception of perfection is the same as God's.

SONG

'You alone are worthy', *Mission Praise*, 2663
'Glory, love and praise', *Hymns Ancient and Modern*, 461
'All I am I offer to you', *Songs of Fellowship*, 2204

WE SAY SORRY

Lord, you alone are perfect and we worship you.

You alone, Lord, are worthy of our praise, not material things coveted nor possessions owned, not philosophies held nor views admired, not even each other – but you alone.

Help us, Lord, to understand our own shortcomings and those of others, to love our neighbours as ourselves, to be compassionate and tolerant and to see the good in all things, for we are all your creation.

Forgive us, Lord, when we place value on things that are valueless in your eyes. Forgive us when we hold dear material possessions, money and status, and remind us that we are all equal in your sight.

In Jesus' name.
Forgive us, we pray.

WE ARE FORGIVEN

Lord, you are the God of Love and you know us. You created us and you understand us like no other.

Bring our hearts back to you, Lord, and let us dwell in your forgiveness.
In Jesus' name.
Amen.

WE AFFIRM OUR FAITH

We believe in one God,
the Father, the Almighty,
maker of heaven and earth,
of all that is, seen and unseen.

We believe in one Lord, Jesus Christ,
the only Son of God,
eternally begotten of the Father,
God from God, Light from Light,
true God from true God,
begotten, not made,

of one Being with the Father.
Through him all things were made.

For us and for our salvation
he came down from heaven:
by the power of the Holy Spirit
he became incarnate from the Virgin Mary,
and was made man.

For our sake he was crucified under Pontius Pilate;
he suffered death and was buried.
On the third day he rose again
in accordance with the Scriptures;
he ascended into heaven
and is seated at the right hand of the Father.

He will come again in glory to judge the living and the dead,
and his kingdom will have no end.

We believe in the Holy Spirit, the Lord, the giver of life,
who proceeds from the Father and the Son.
With the Father and the Son he is worshipped and glorified.
He has spoken through the Prophets.
We believe in one holy catholic and apostolic Church.
We acknowledge one baptism for the forgiveness of sins.
We look for the resurrection of the dead,
and the life of the world to come.
Amen.

SONG

'A new commandment I give to you', *Mission Praise*, 1
'All creatures of our God and King', *Hymns Ancient and Modern*, 105
'Who is this love amazing?', *Songs of Fellowship*, 2657

READING

Philippians 2.2–8

> then make my joy complete by being like-minded, having the same love, being one in spirit and of one mind. Do nothing out of selfish ambition or vain conceit. Rather, in humility value others above yourselves, not looking to your own interests but each of you to the interests of the others.
>
> In your relationships with one another, have the same mindset as Christ Jesus:
>
> who, being in very nature God,
>> did not consider equality with God something to be used to his own advantage;
>> rather, he made himself nothing
>>> by taking the very nature of a servant,
>>> being made in human likeness.
>> And being found in appearance as a man,
>>> he humbled himself
>>> by becoming obedient to death – even death on a cross!

TALK

If you are like me then you spend many hours trying to make things right: the perfect party, the perfect home, the perfect outfit, maybe – even the perfect sermon.

But what is perfect and how do we judge it – and would God agree?

I'd like you, please, to look around you and collect a fallen leaf. The best that you can find.

Allow some time for this to happen.

Now examine the leaf that you have chosen.
Is it whole?
Complete, possessing all its parts?
Does it have a good colour?
Does it look nice?
Is it as good a leaf as you can find?
Now throw that leaf away and find another, one that is not perfect.

Again allow some time for this to happen.

Now sit and hold this leaf in your hands. Look at its shape; visualize how it once used to look and think of the journeys that it has been through to make it this way.

Now wash the leaf in the water.

Pass the bucket and towel around for people to do this and then dry their hands.

Now see how it looks. Hold it carefully so as not to damage it more.

Now look really closely at the veins that you can see and imagine how once they caught the sun and fed the plant. See how perfectly made the leaf is – how well suited to its function, how delicate its gentle decay.

This leaf will crumble further until it is no longer recognizable. It will be subsumed into the earth and will become part of new life in months and years to come.

How much more perfect can this example of life be?

I would like to ask you to hold someone in your mind now.

Someone who perhaps irritates you or wears you down, someone you consider to be very far from perfect.

I would like to ask you to consider if God considers that person perfect.

What does he hold valuable in his children?

Does he love them as much as he loves you?

Now look again at your leaf, washed clean and showing the signs of a life well lived, a life in service to God's creation.

Put the leaf back somewhere on the ground, somewhere sheltered if you like, where it can continue its journey and complete the perfect purpose for which God created it.

God has a purpose for all people and all things.

He has a purpose for us – for you.

Who are we to determine what is and is not perfect? By loving and trusting God we are perfect in his sight, and he asks no more of us than to be the best we can be in him – for him that is perfection.

As we go through the next few weeks, let us be gentle on ourselves and others when we or they fail to meet our expectations or live up to our standards.

God created us to be flawed, to be imperfect. To look to him for redemption. To be washed clean of our sin by his holy word.

WE SHARE THE PEACE

We come together as one family, one worshipping congregation. All different and all unique in God's holy eyes.

God gave us peace through knowing him and this peace we share with one another.
Let us greet one another with a sign of that peace.

SONG

'All heaven declares', *Mission Praise*, 14
'Lord, teach us how to pray aright', *Hymns Ancient and Modern*, 227
'Who is this love amazing?', *Songs of Fellowship*, 2657

During this song a collection may be taken.

WE PRAY TOGETHER

Lord, you are perfect.
Make us a tolerant people, Lord, a people of compassion and forgiveness.
Forgive us that we too may forgive others.
Lord, remind us that we are your children and your people and that by your grace we live.
Lord, in your mercy,
Hear our prayer.

Lord, we pray for all those in public office who have the burden of decision-making upon them. Show them that no decision is perfect unless made with you in mind.
Lord, in your mercy,
Hear our prayer.

Lord, we pray for all those who are unwell in mind or in body.
Give them your peace, Father, and grant them rest and healing.
Lord, in your mercy,
Hear our prayer.

Lord, we pray for those who are homeless, for those who are cast out, for those who live in fear and for those whose journeys are so much harder than our own.

Comfort and guide them, Lord. Help us to open our hearts to their plight and grant them courage.

Lord, in your mercy,

Hear our prayer.

Together we say the Lord's Prayer.

Our Father in heaven
Hallowed be your name.
Your kingdom come
Your will be done
On earth as it is in heaven.
Give us today our daily bread
And forgive us our trespasses
As we forgive those who trespass against us.
Lead us not into temptation
But deliver us from evil.
For the kingdom, the power and the glory are yours
Now and for ever.
Amen.

WE GO INTO THE WORLD TOGETHER

So go out into the world today with a more tender heart, a more forgiving nature.

To be better reflections of God in the world.

For this is our function and our purpose for which he created us.

We go out together to love and serve the Lord.

Thanks be to God.

Remembrance

SERVICE

Focus: Understanding the importance of remembering and making time to remember.

Resources:

- A length of ribbon for every person.
- Access to a tree or a structure that you can tie the ribbons to.

WE GATHER FOR WORSHIP

Today we gather together in remembrance. To recall those that we have loved and lost, those who have made sacrifices for us, and also to remember the many and great blessings bestowed upon us.

We will remember the times in our own lives when we have had cause to be thankful and we will reflect upon them.

SONG

'Bind us together, Lord', *Mission Praise*, 54
'Lord, save thy world', *Hymns Ancient and Modern*, 397
'Empires fall but you're still standing', *Songs of Fellowship*, 2264

WE SAY SORRY

Lord, often we fall short of the standards of the world – but more importantly, Lord, we fall short of your standards.

We open our hearts now to the times when we have not been all that we could be, when we have not lived up to our potential in you.
Whether through laziness, fear or carelessness.

We recognize, Lord, that we are not always grateful and that we take our ease, our freedom and our comfort too much for granted as we turn our eyes from the plight of others.
Forgive us, Lord, and make us newly wondrous of your great goodness.
Amen.

WE ARE FORGIVEN

Heavenly Father, who knows only too well our shortcomings, thank you that you make us new in your sight.

Strengthen us, Lord, as we resolve to do better and try harder. Bless us as we go forward forgiven.

In Jesus' name.
Amen.

WE AFFIRM OUR FAITH

We believe in one God,
the Father, the Almighty,
maker of heaven and earth,
of all that is, seen and unseen.

We believe in one Lord, Jesus Christ,
the only Son of God,
eternally begotten of the Father,
God from God, Light from Light,
true God from true God,
begotten, not made,
of one Being with the Father.
Through him all things were made.

For us and for our salvation
he came down from heaven:
by the power of the Holy Spirit

he became incarnate from the Virgin Mary,
and was made man.

For our sake he was crucified under Pontius Pilate;
he suffered death and was buried.
On the third day he rose again
in accordance with the Scriptures;
he ascended into heaven
and is seated at the right hand of the Father.

He will come again in glory to judge the living and the dead,
and his kingdom will have no end.

We believe in the Holy Spirit, the Lord, the giver of life,
who proceeds from the Father and the Son.
With the Father and the Son he is worshipped and glorified.
He has spoken through the Prophets.
We believe in one holy catholic and apostolic Church.
We acknowledge one baptism for the forgiveness of sins.
We look for the resurrection of the dead,
and the life of the world to come.
Amen.

SONG

'In Christ alone my hope is found', *Mission Praise*, 1072
'We turn to you, O God', *Hymns Ancient and Modern*, 522
'God is our strength and refuge', *Songs of Fellowship*, 2296

READINGS

1 Chronicles 16.12–15

Remember the wonders he has done,
     his miracles, and the judgments he pronounced,
you his servants, the descendants of Israel,
     his chosen ones, the children of Jacob.
He is the Lord our God;
     his judgments are in all the earth.
He remembers his covenant for ever,
     the promise he made, for a thousand generations.

Deuteronomy 6.10–15 (ESV)

And when the Lord your God brings you into the land that he swore to your fathers, to Abraham, to Isaac, and to Jacob, to give you – with great and good cities that you did not build, and houses full of all good things that you did not fill, and cisterns that you did not dig, and vineyards and olive trees that you did not plant – and when you eat and are full, then take care lest you forget the Lord, who brought you out of the land of Egypt, out of the house of slavery. It is the Lord your God you shall fear. Him you shall serve and by his name you shall swear.

TALK

When we are submersed in the busy-ness of our day-to-day lives – the school run, the commute to work, the tasks around the home and family that need to be addressed – it can be difficult to take time to reflect and remember.

The act of remembering is something that requires discipline and focus. It requires you to think back, to search through the pockets of your mind and recall a time, an event, a person.

Remembering is important. It is how we learn from mistakes, it is how we keep with us a sense of loved ones departed, it is how we retain hope when hope can seem lost, and it is how we recall the times when God was with us and saved us.

On a personal level it is how we better ourselves and become more reflective and seek God.

On a global level it is how we learn from the atrocities of the past and how we seek solutions to the atrocities of the present.

As we grow older, remembering is a valuable tool, a vehicle to keep us rooted in a sense of place and time, a reassurance of a life well lived and a comfort in the long slow hours.

We must not forget to remember.

But it can take time, and time is a precious commodity in our hurried lives.

Sometimes it helps to have a visual reminder of something – a modern-day knotted handkerchief.

Sometimes we have to make a time for remembering, a time for looking back and learning from the past. A time to allow ourselves to feel again the warmth of a lost memory, the power of a meaningful recollection. Sometimes the act of remembering one thing will open doors in our minds to other things previously unremembered.

I'd like you to take your ribbon now and think of a memory you would like to associate with that ribbon. It doesn't have to be particularly happy or sad, it doesn't even have to be that meaningful.

It might be a recollection of an activity, an experience or a person. It might be a conscious effort to feel again the way you felt when you were younger, it might be an effort to see a loved one's face again and look into their eyes, it might be wanting to remember how it felt to have faith.

Once you have decided on your memory, please come up to the tree and tie your ribbon on, making that an active tool for reflection. As you tie the ribbon, work hard in your mind to remember what it symbolizes. Do not allow anything else to interrupt that.

As you step away, look at your ribbon and the ribbons of others.

So many memories and so many thoughts, tied up in so many emotions for some.

And yet our Father God knows every single one of these.

Think about where God was in your life when this memory was being formed.

>Was he with you?
>Were you adrift?
>Did you look to him?
>Were you angry with him, perhaps?
>How does it feel to know that he was there?
>He was there.
>When that memory was being formed and every moment before and after?
>How often do we reflect on how often God has been there for us?
>Next to us.
>Loving us.

WE SHARE THE PEACE

Let us come together remembering God's great love for us.
Let us share the sign of the peace in remembrance of others.

SONG

'Praise God from whom all blessing flow', *Mission Praise*, 1348
'There is God's garden', *Hymns Ancient and Modern*, 514
'Our God forever', *Songs of Fellowship*, 2493

WE PRAY TOGETHER

Lord, you are a God of great gifts. So often we forget the blessings that you
have given us and the peace and comfort that have surrounded us in our times
of need.
Father, we thank you now.
Lord, in your mercy,
Hear our prayer.

Father, we praise and thank you, we remember your kindness and great mercy
and we ask your forgiveness that we do not set aside time more often to reflect
upon your great goodness.
Lord, forgive us.
Lord, in your mercy,
Hear our prayer.

Lord, help us to remember that you are there for us always and that your love
does not falter but grows stronger with every thought and deed in your name.
Lord, remind us of your love.
Lord, in your mercy,
Hear our prayer.

Truly, Lord, you are a God of miracles, a God who does not forget.
Remind us, Father, of the need to reflect upon you and upon our lives.
You gave us, Lord, the gift of recall that we may improve ourselves and be of
comfort to others.
You gave us, Lord, the gift of recall that we may better love you and remember
you in our lives.

We remember those who are or were important to us, those we loved, those who loved us. And Lord, we remember all the times in our lives when you saved us.
In Jesus' name.
Amen.

Together we say the Lord's Prayer.
Our Father in heaven
Hallowed be your name.
Your kingdom come
Your will be done
On earth as it is in heaven.
Give us today our daily bread
And forgive us our trespasses
As we forgive those who trespass against us.
Lead us not into temptation
But deliver us from evil.
For the kingdom, the power and the glory are yours
Now and for ever.
Amen.

WE GO INTO THE WORLD TOGETHER

So as we leave this place and head into our busy week, may we be blessed with a moment to remember.
And through remembering may we better know our God.
And by better knowing our God may we bring greater light to the world.
In the name of Christ.
Amen.

Words and pictures

In this activity participants use autumnal natural materials to create words and pictures that can be displayed either inside or outside the church. This could be an opportunity to encourage the wider community to visit your church to see your display.

Focus: Nature as an inspiration and as a material to share a message.
Type of activity: Part of an activity for a specific group or the whole church community.
Age range: The whole church family.
Resources:
- Natural materials found around you. If you don't have much in your immediate surroundings that you can collect, organizers can gather materials beforehand.
- Bags, baskets or boxes to collect your materials in.
- While you may decide to use only natural materials in your construction, horticultural wire or twine can be a useful addition, in which case you will also need something to cut it with.

Aim

The aim of the session is for everyone to use natural materials to express something important – creating words or pictures that express a particular message.

Structure

Discussion as a group
The outdoors bit
Bringing it all together

Discussion as a group

Depending on the size of your group, you could work all together or split into groups. This description assumes that you will do the latter.

Choose an overall theme, such as harvest or Christian virtues. Each group can work either on the overall theme or on one specific element within it, e.g. the word 'Love'.

Take a look at the work of Stefan Sagmeister (specifically his typography) and Andy Goldsworthy as inspiration. These artists both use natural materials to create their art, in ways that are achievable by non-artists. There are examples on the website too.

The outdoors bit

Each group will need to decide whether they are going to make a word or an image and also where they are going to display their art. Will the artworks all be displayed outside, all inside or a mixture of the two?

Participants should begin by collecting the materials they wish to use to create their artworks, then work together to design and develop their finished pieces. Using the natural materials they have collected, the artworks should form words or pictures that express a message for others to read.

To form words, bend sticks and wind foliage around them to create letters. These can then be displayed in trees, against a wall or fence or on the ground. (See colour photos of 'Hope' and 'Joy' on the website.)

Branches and leaves forming 'Hope' and 'Joy'

Your pictures can be representational or express a theme (see colour photo of 'September scene' on the website). Or you can create abstract patterns. The stunning colours of autumn leaves can be formed into lines of colour, from light to darker shades, or rainbows.

September scene

The images might be displayed close to where the materials have been found, towards the front of the church grounds for others to see, or brought inside the church (see 'Bringing the outside in' in the first section of the book).

While this activity can take place at any time of year, autumnal colours are particularly effective.

Bringing it all together

Take photographs of the outdoor art and display them inside so that all members of the church community can see what has been achieved. These images can also be used in services alongside songs or readings, about harvest or any other theme you have chosen.

You could invite other members of the local community to come and view your art. If you display them towards the front of the church's grounds people passing by will see them too.

Winter

An Advent adventure

Children create their own nativity scenes. First they make stables out of cardboard boxes. Then they visit the houses of members of the church community to collect from behind these 'Advent doors', and then colour in, the figures to go inside.

Focus: Preparing for Christmas by making individual nativity scenes while making links between the different generations within the church community.

Type of activity: Family fun day or Sunday school, followed by an outdoor, after-school (or weekend) activity.

Age range: Everyone in the church community can be involved.

Resources:

- Cardboard boxes, straw (or similar), paint (brown, grey and blue) and paint brushes, extra cardboard, gold coloured paper, scissors and glue.
- Blue tissue or translucent plastic, sticky stars.
- Thin white card for using to make the figures for the stable. (See illustration on p. 36.)
- Instructions for all those taking part.
- A list of the houses to be visited, and when.

Aim

The aim of this activity is for individual children or families to create their own nativity scenes. The stables are made at a group activity, and the figures are collected by going to visit members of the local community in their homes, behind their 'Advent doors'.

This can be started at a family event (such as an Advent tea) or for the children only at Sunday school or a similar event. The outdoors bit follows later.

Structure

Initial planning
Making the stables
Getting ready for the visits
The outdoors bit
To finish off

Initial planning

The first task is to find out who in your church community is willing and able to welcome visitors to their house, to host an 'Advent door'. Whoever hosts a door will need to be at home at a set time for the children's visits. This could be just an hour on one evening, so it is not too onerous for people to take part. Plan when you will visit the houses, the start and the finish and the route to be taken.

This is a great way for younger members of the congregation to get to know older or infirm members of your church, maybe people who cannot attend church very often. You will probably find that many people in your congregation will love to have the children to visit.

Making the stable

Arrange a session that brings everyone together to create the stables. Gather together enough cardboard boxes so that each child or family can create a stable. If you would like windows in your stables it is a good idea to cut these out beforehand so that the time you have can be spent on decorating the stables.

Lay out plastic sheeting or newspapers so that you create places to work without getting paint on the church floor. Provide paint in browns, greys and blues, and paint brushes or small shapes of sponge that can be dipped into the paint (this

Making stables

makes less of a mess). You will also need tabs of cardboard – about 10cm by 5cm – to stick the main star on to and some glue. Blue tissue paper or translucent plastic (cut to just bigger than your windows) can be used to create window panes. In addition supply small sticky stars for the sky and a large star to hover over your stable.

Each child or family creates their own stable. Paint the cardboard tab blue and stick the large star on it, then secure this to the top of the stable, as seen in the picture. Then decorate the rest of the stable – painting the inside and adding texture to the roof with straw or wool. (See colour photo of making stables on the website.)

Getting ready for the visits

The leaders need to create line draw- ings of all the characters that go into each stable. You can use the images provided to make a sheet of outlines of all the characters you need. Use thin white card for your characters and cut out extra strips about 2cm by 10cm. Fold the strips into three sections, with the central third attached to the back of the figures and the two ends folded backwards to make them stand up. (See colour photo of advent adventure structure on the website.)

Advent adventure structure

Distribute the characters among the houses to be visited (e.g. if you are visiting four houses, split the characters into four groups) so that the children get all the characters they need with no duplicates. (See illustrations on the website.)

When these figures have been collected the children will colour them in and place into each stable.

Your key characters are:

- Mary
- Joseph
- Jesus (to be handed out at your Christmas Eve or Christmas Day service)
- Angels
- Shepherds
- Sheep
- Donkey
- Cattle
- Any other animals such as chickens, geese, goats

The outdoors bit

At the prearranged time, your children and parents should meet at your church, ready to go on the visits. Depending on the numbers you have you could split the group so that not too many people turn up at each door at the same time. Leaders take the groups to each house in turn and knock on the 'Advent doors'.

The residents of the houses hand out the required number of figures needed for each stable, so that when all the houses have been visited everyone's set is complete. The children take away their figures, colour them in and stand them up in their stable. In this way each child or family ends up creating their own nativity scene.

To finish off

Make some extra sets of figures so that you can hand these out to anyone who did not attend the visiting session, maybe at a Christingle service or on Christmas Day. You also need to hand out the baby Jesus at this time – so that he only appears in the nativity scenes on Christmas Day itself. (See colour photo of advent adventure final scene on the website.)

Advent adventure final scene

Christingle

SERVICE

Focus: Christingle service focusing on the world and the needs of others.
Resources:
Items representing the different parts of a Christingle:
• Your church takes the place of the orange.
• A Christingle lantern represents the candle (see below for instructions).
• A long ribbon to go around your church represents the love and blood of Christ (see below for different options for this).
• An apple tree ready to be planted, represents the fruit and sweets, symbols of God's creation.

As the activity is fairly long, the service is aimed at children and the weather is likely to be chilly, the service is slightly shorter than others in this book. More songs can be added if required ('He's got the whole world in his hands' is a good song that fits with the Christingle message but traditional carols can also be used). Other more traditional Christingle readings could be used, for example:

Isaiah 9.2–4, 6–7
Matthew 1.18–23
John 1.1–5

WELCOME

The Christingle service is an opportunity to reflect upon our place in the world and on the needs of others.

It is also a chance for us to get to know more about Jesus and how we as Christians choose to live our lives.

OPENING PRAYER

Lord, as we gather today in your wonderful world we thank you for the many blessings you bestow upon us.

We thank you that we can stand here on this cold night but remain warm and safe, and we think of those for whom the cold winter brings fear and pain.

We think of those who need your light, Lord, in these dark days, and those who cannot find comfort in friendships but sit alone.

Let us reflect, Lord, on our great good fortune and seek to honour you by sharing what we have with those who are in need.

Remind us that we need to be your light in this world, and through us can be reflected the face of God.

SONG

'Away in a manger', *Mission Praise*, 47
'Hark the herald angels sing', *Mission Praise*, 211
'Angels from the realms of glory', *Hymns Ancient and Modern*, 39

READING

This is most effective if read by a child:
    So here I stand, . . ., one girl among many.
    I speak – not for myself, but for all girls and boys.
    I raise up my voice – not so that I can shout, but so that those without a voice
    can be heard.
    Those who have fought for their rights:
    Their right to live in peace.
    Their right to be treated with dignity.
    Their right to equality of opportunity.
    Their right to be educated.

Dear sisters and brothers, we realize the importance of light when we see darkness. We realize the importance of our voice when we are silenced.

TALK

Does anyone know who made this powerful speech?

Invite people to respond.

This is a speech made by Malala Yousafzai to the United Nations and it reminds us never to take for granted the things that we have in this world and our privileged place in it.
As we reflect upon our place in the world I am going to ask you to look up at the sky.
As you look up let your eyes be drawn to the vastness of the universe.
Use these moments to remind yourself that you are one of many, part of a greater whole, and together with others your faith will shine more brightly than if you were alone.

You might like to consider the image of the London 2012 Olympic cauldron which was made up of many individual 'petals' – each containing a light. Together they shone brighter than each light shining on their own.

This is why we come together.
This is why we are Church.
Feel the might and the majesty of the skies and understand how small you are within that space. Let perspective realign what is important to you and be in awe of how much you are loved by your Father even though you are so small in his creation.
Now bring your eyes down again and look around at each other.
This is your Church and you are light in the world.

Light the Christingle lantern – see below for instructions on making a lantern.

As we light this lantern consider how you reflect God's light, how you honour him in your thoughts, words and deeds.
Ask forgiveness for the times when your thoughts, words or deeds were not worthy of him. Repent and resolve to try harder.
You have all prepared a length of ribbon. The ribbon is red; this symbolizes Jesus' blood shed for us – the ultimate sacrifice.
We are going to move around the church building now and tie the lengths of ribbon together. As we do so, look at what others have attached to their ribbons – their views of the church in the world.

Depending on the size of your congregation, involve everyone, or as many people as you need, in preparing lengths of ribbon, attaching pictures and images to them. Before the service, measure the circumference of the church and work out how much ribbon you will need. See below for ways to make your ribbon.

If you've got plenty of time:

As we come back together, take a look at the ribbon that you have tied around the church. In doing this you have bound the church into service to others, you have acknowledged our role in the world and we have committed to share our blessings.

We will now give thanks for the fruits of the Spirit. In a traditional Christingle service we would use this time to attach dried fruit to our oranges, but this time we are going to plant a symbol of hope and sustenance for the future.

We are going to plant an apple tree.

See below on how to plant an apple tree. Invite one or two members of the congregation to plant the tree.

SONG

'The first nowell', *Mission Praise*, 664
'It came upon the midnight clear', *Hymns Ancient and Modern*, 41

PRAYERS

Lord, you give us light and peace and hope.
You give us a world in which to live.
You give us the fruits of the Spirit that we may reflect your light in this world.
You feed us and clothe us, you give us your unconditional love.
We thank you for your grace and mercy.
We thank you for your patience.
We thank you that you give us each other for comfort and for friendship.
We promise that we will be your lights in this world, that we will think of others before ourselves, that we will notice those in need this Christmas and throughout the year.
That we will remember you daily, honour you always and love you for ever.
Amen.

Making your Christingle lantern

The lantern takes the place of the candle – which represents Jesus as the light of the world. This type of lantern can be 'planted' in the ground and left in place for the length of the service. (See colour photo of home-made lantern on the website.)

Home-made lantern

You will need:

- A broom handle or similar length of wood.
- A sharp knife.
- A small empty tuna tin and a large empty tuna tin.
- A nail and a hammer.
- Screws and a screwdriver.
- A glass that fits snugly inside your large tuna tin.
- Metallic paint.
- A candle and matches.

Putting it together:

- Cut one end of your pole into a point. Make sure the other end is flat.
- Hammer a hole into the middle of the large tuna tin using your nail – you will need to be able to drive a screw through this hole.
- The smaller tin needs to have the pole running through it. Make a star shape of holes, which will allow you to bend the tin to poke the pole through. Push the blunt end of the pole upwards through the tin so that the sharp edges work their way inwards. Push the tin down the pole so that the top of this tin is level with the top of the pole.
- Make two holes in the side of this tin, and push screws through them, which are secured into the wooden pole, fixing the tin in place.
- The larger tin is then placed on top and secured by a screw driven through the middle into the top of the pole.
- Paint the whole structure with metallic paint. Add the glass when the paint is dry.
- Shorten your candle so that it burns within the glass. Melt the bottom end of your candle, letting the wax drip into the glass. Use this to secure the candle in the lantern.

- Stick the lantern into the ground. Make sure it is stable, then it is ready to be lit.

Making your ribbon

The red ribbon indicates the love and blood of Christ.

- You could simply use one long length of red florist's ribbon, to which you attach pictures of the church in the world as part of the service.
- An old sheet or duvet cover could be torn into strips about 10cm wide. A king-sized duvet will provide you with about 200m of ribbon. If you don't have red sheets(!) you will need to dye the strips ahead of time. This type of ribbon can have images attached to it too.
- Or you could make up your 'ribbon' using strips of paper (wallpaper lining paper cut in half lengthways is ideal). Sections of this can be decorated by members of the church, with the aim of making the colour an overall red, so they could paint sections plain red or use different shades of red for illustrations. Connect the strips together to give the impression of a long red ribbon. This can be the activity within the service.

Planting your apple tree

This represents the fruit and sweets, which are symbols of God's creation and the seasons.

- Make sure that if this is the only apple tree in the planting area that it is self-fertile.
- If you haven't got much space, the tree could be planted against a fence or hedge and trained as an espalier or cordon.
- In advance prepare a deep enough hole for the tree and have a spade and some loose earth ready. If the weather is cold and you are purchasing your tree sometime before the service, be sure to choose one that is container grown, as this will protect the roots during frosty weather.
- Plant the tree so that the soil is level with the original planted depth, and be sure to keep it well watered for the first year. Smaller trees may need staking or other protection – your local garden centre can advise you.
- It is a good idea to keep the base of your tree weed-free for up to five years to encourage it to grow. Regularly check your tree tie and support so that it doesn't damage the stem of your tree.

Following in the footsteps of the wise men

A walk going from the east towards your church, remembering the journey of the wise men and undertaking some simple activities related to the story on the way.

Focus: To consider the journey of the wise men at Epiphany.
Type of activity: A pilgrimage for your church community or a group within it.
Age range: All ages and groups. This activity could be planned by your teenagers for younger members of your church community.
Resources:
- A compass (most smart phones will have one).
- A map of your local area.
- Map materials – wallpaper lining paper, coloured pens/paints and paint brushes, camera/camera phone, printer, paper, scissors and glue.
- Items to represent gold, frankincense and myrrh (see below for ideas).
- A large jam tart in the shape of a six-point star with either a hard bean or a golden ring hidden in it.
- Dressing-up costumes for three kings or queens.
- Chalk, or glow chalk and a torch.

Aim

To consider the journey of the wise men and to plan and undertake your own pilgrimage, drawing on traditions of the Epiphany from around the world.

Structure

The outdoors bit
   Planning the journey
   Your journey
When you arrive

The outdoors bit

Planning the journey

The initial part of this activity consists of all the important planning for the journey.

The route needs to be planned well ahead of Epiphany. Create an annotated map giving directions and instructions for your journey. This can be done by one group within the church for other groups to follow, such as your young people planning for the younger children.

Start by taking a map of your local area that includes the location of your church. Then choose a starting point for the journey that is somewhere east of your church, so that your journey is roughly in a westerly direction, just like that of the magi. This needs to be within two or three miles of your final destination, depending on the stamina and mobility of those who will go on the journey.

Those who are planning this activity will be required to walk the route themselves in advance. They then should draw the route map, showing the activities to be included on the way. Remember that you are travelling due west in as straight a line as you can. Your map can be created using a roll of wallpaper lining paper to show the route as you travel. This can be unrolled and rolled up as your group undertakes the actual journey. (See illustration of the journey on the website.) The map should include:

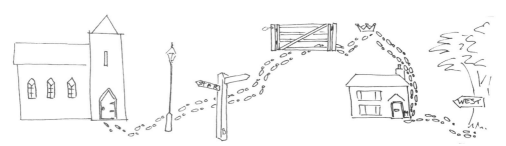

Journey of the wise men

- The path of the route – this could be indicated by footprints on your map, for example, or a line of crowns. Your young people may come up with their own ideas for how to do this.
- The points of activity or other points marked on the route.

- Images of some features on the route to look out for on the journey. These could be photographs or drawings.
- Any particular instructions, such as information about where to meet Herod and where to collect the kings' gifts.

Your activities undertaken on the way can be based on traditions from around the world that are associated with Epiphany. In some countries this time is known as 'the three kings days' (or a similar title). Ideas for some activities, together with elements of the story of the three wise men, are detailed below.

A reminder of the order of events in the Bible story:

- See the star rising in the west and start the journey.
- Visit Herod in Jerusalem.
- Carry on to Bethlehem.
- Find Mary, Joseph and Jesus, and present the gifts.
- Being warned in a dream not to return to Herod and go back a different route.

On the day, everyone should meet at the beginning point ready for your pilgrimage.

Your journey

Before you start, begin by sharing a large jam tart in the shape of a six-pointed star (an old English tradition). In the tart is hidden either a bean that has been baked hard or a gold ring. The tart is divided up by one of the younger members of the church quite randomly, then shared out. The person who finds the bean or ring is king or queen for the day. Or you could hide three items, so that you end up with three kings/queens.

Some of your group can be dressed up as kings/queens for the journey to represent the three kings (this happens in Goa and Germany, for example).

In some countries (such as Poland) chalk is used to write the initials of the three kings (traditionally Balthazar, Caspar and Melchior) on places or things passed on the journey, for instance above the doors of local houses. Those planning the journey need to write the initials in advance on various places or objects that will be passed by. Choose three places, one for each king, where the corresponding gift will be 'found'. In the countryside this might be on rocks, gate posts or tree trunks; in a more urban area this might be at points on a path. Mark on your map where these will be, so that those following the route can look out for them.

If you are undertaking your pilgrimage in the dark you can use glow chalk. This is chalk soaked in water coloured by ink from the inside of a highlighter pen, then left to dry. The chalk becomes fluorescent and the writing can be picked out by the use of a torch with an ultra violet beam.

At each place where you have marked a king's initials the corresponding gift representing gold, frankincense and myrrh will be collected. Your young people can perhaps look after the gifts beforehand, then the younger children can collect them when you arrive at the particular locations.

Suggestions for items to represent the gifts:

- Gold – represents the kingship of Jesus:
  - golden flowers such as mahonia (this flowers from November to March)
  - pebbles painted gold
  - a crown or sceptre, something that represents royalty
- Frankincense – his priestly role:
  - pine resin
  - aromatic herbs
  - something 'priestly', such as a crook or a prayer book
- Myrrh – prefiguring his death (it is used for embalming):
  - a tree resin
  - scented wax
  - a cross, foretelling Jesus' death

There are some other activities that can be included on your journey:

- Take a lantern with you to represent the star.
- Visit King Herod. Decide where Jerusalem will be on your journey and mark this on the map. Someone should act out being King Herod and ask the kings where they are going and what they are doing. They tell him about their journey and he asks them to come back and tell him what they find.
- Collect some grass or hay and water for the kings' camels.
- Sing some songs as you walk, about stars or the kings/wise men.

SONG

'We three kings of orient are', *Hymns Old and New*, Complete Anglican
  Edition, 740

'As with gladness men of old', *Hymns Old and New*, Complete Anglican
   Edition, 50
'Wonder of a newborn son', *Songs of Fellowship*, 2661

When you arrive

- When you arrive at your church at the end of your journey, take down your Christmas decorations. Any foliage you have used can be burnt on a bonfire (see the health and safety section for advice about working with fire) or composted.
- You can add models of the kings, or the gifts you have collected, to your nativity scene.
- Finish your journey with a feast of foods from around the world used to celebrate Epiphany. See below for some ideas of what to serve.
- Ask people to go home by a different route, as the kings were warned in a dream to return a different way.

Some food and drink for your feast:

- **Drink** – in English Wassail traditions mulled cider is served on Twelfth Night. You could replace this with warmed spiced apple juice that everyone can drink.
- **Sweets** – handed out to children in various places around the world when they visit houses and sing songs – in a very similar way to carol singing.
- **Twelfth Night cake** – a fruit cake that was traditionally made in England.
- **Spiced cookies** – made in Finland, for example.
- **A special cake or bread** – baked in Wales, this is divided into three parts, representing Christ, Mary and the wise men. Rings are concealed in the cake or loaf, and whoever finds one is elected as a king or queen for the day.

Light and dark

SERVICE

Focus: Celebrating and embracing the darkness as the herald of light and new life. Thinking about how we approach and support those in our community who feel consumed by darkness.

Resources:

- Somewhere outside for people to sit, as this service has a more traditional format.
- A place where you can light a small fire; a free-standing fire pit would be perfect for this.
- A candle of some description for each member of the congregation: perhaps a tea light in a jam jar or a small candle pushed through a circle of paper or card to catch falling wax.
- A few sheets of newspaper.
- Matches.

WE GATHER FOR WORSHIP

Welcome to our service of light and dark. Tonight we focus our thoughts on the light of the world that is our Lord Jesus Christ and the faith that he instils within us.

We will think about our role in the world and how we sometimes strive to be all things to everyone with our own small light, and fail – but how together we will burn more brightly than we ever could alone.

SONG

'Lord, the light of your love is shining', *Mission Praise*, 445
'Christ is the world's light', *Hymns Ancient and Modern*, 440
'And can it be that I should gain', *Songs of Fellowship*, 2215

WE SAY SORRY

Lord, so often we step out on our own, and in our own power, to try and fix things, make things right, correct wrongs or campaign against an injustice. So often we set ourselves impossible tasks and then condemn ourselves when we fail to achieve them.

Lord, forgive us for not trusting in you, for not resting in your power and walking in the path of your leadership.
Father, when we exalt our own strength above yours.
Forgive us.

When we turn inwards to seek answers to problems before looking to you.
Forgive us.

When we take glory in achievements only made possible by your grace.
Forgive us.

And for when we try to make our own light burn brighter, forgetting to join with our brothers and sisters.
Forgive us.

WE ARE FORGIVEN

Our Lord Jesus Christ came to death on the cross for the forgiveness of our wrongdoings. He rose again as permanent proof of his great mercy.

Every day as we go about our busy lives, and forget that we do so only by the grace of his great mercy, he forgives us again and again for our transgressions.

Every time we pray and worship together he gives us his light, that we may go forth into the world as a new family.

Father, thank you that your light reveals your mercy and casts our sin into darkness.

WE AFFIRM OUR FAITH

We believe in one God,
the Father, the Almighty,
maker of heaven and earth,
of all that is, seen and unseen.

We believe in one Lord, Jesus Christ,
the only Son of God,
eternally begotten of the Father,
God from God, Light from Light,
true God from true God,
begotten, not made,
of one Being with the Father.
Through him all things were made.

For us and for our salvation
he came down from heaven:
by the power of the Holy Spirit
he became incarnate from the Virgin Mary,
and was made man.

For our sake he was crucified under Pontius Pilate;
he suffered death and was buried.
On the third day he rose again
in accordance with the Scriptures;
he ascended into heaven
and is seated at the right hand of the Father.

He will come again in glory to judge the living and the dead,
and his kingdom will have no end.

We believe in the Holy Spirit, the Lord, the giver of life,
who proceeds from the Father and the Son.
With the Father and the Son he is worshipped and glorified.
He has spoken through the Prophets.
We believe in one holy catholic and apostolic Church.
We acknowledge one baptism for the forgiveness of sins.
We look for the resurrection of the dead,
and the life of the world to come.
Amen.

SONG

'All earth was dark until you spoke', *Mission Praise*, 8
'Christ is the world's true light', *Hymns Ancient and Modern*, 346
'Who I have become in you', *Songs of Fellowship*, 2655

READINGS

2 Corinthians 4.6

For God, who said, 'Let light shine out of darkness,' made his light shine in our hearts to give us the light of the knowledge of God's glory displayed in the face of Christ.

John 1.1–9

In the beginning was the Word, and the Word was with God, and the Word was God. He was with God in the beginning. Through him all things were made; without him nothing was made that has been made. In him was life, and that life was the light of all mankind. The light shines in the darkness, and the darkness has not overcome it.

There was a man sent from God whose name was John. He came as a witness to testify concerning that light, so that through him all might believe. He himself was not the light; he came only as a witness to the light.

The true light that gives light to everyone was coming into the world.

TALK

I'd like us to take a moment to contemplate the dark, to see how it surrounds us. As you look around you, notice how the space beyond the lights is even darker and how thick the blackness seems to be.

As you read the following passage create a small fire in the fire pit with newspaper and matches. Don't use anything other than newspaper as the aim is that the fire will blaze brightly and then go out very quickly.

Once there were many in the darkness.
Afraid and alone.
One came who promised great light.
A light that would never go out.
A light that would take away all fear.
One man.
And in exchange he demanded exaltation and honour.

And then also came one who did not promise this, one who gave man to man,
each to each other, and promised them eternal life in him.
In each faithful heart he lit a candle flame of faith.
The one who promised great light built a vast fire,
the flames leapt to the heavens and gave great warmth.
Many exalted him and called him wonderful.
The light blazed and then, after a short time, was gone.
And could not be relit.
And the many were cold and in the dark again.
The one who gave man to man and promised eternal life and
who lit the flame in each humble heart prompted each to look to each other
and draw from his divine glory.
Each small flame relit another as one went out.
And the sum of them was never diminished.
For together God made us stronger.

Towards the end of the passage, each member of the congregation should have their small candle lit. The easiest way to do this is for the person at the end of each row to light their candle, then the next person's candle, then everyone lights each other's – this also reflects the narrative well.

It's so tempting as humans to want to be the one who creates the big blaze, finds the answer to the problem and is praised for it.

But this is not God's way.
His is the way of small deeds and quiet humility, humble acts carried out in private.
He gave us each other that we might constantly help and encourage and grow our faith together.

There are many symbols and reflections of darkness in our communities and we all have a role to play in bringing light to these.
For some the very real darkness of sadness or depression surrounds them and it is hard to watch strong people be consumed by this.

Never forget that we can help relight each other's faith but that we do not do this in our own power.
We must pray and be watchful and wait on God to help us find the right way.

At this time of year especially many people suffer from sadness. The long nights are filled with lonely and painful hours and these pass slowly.

It is not always easy to see those that suffer for they exist in their own private darkness and often do not welcome others into that.

But small gestures of light, small gifts of time or caring can help.
Even in the darkest of days we can be light.
Often it is tempting to say, 'I don't know what to do to help', or 'I am so frustrated that I can't do something', or 'I feel so badly for you'.
All of these sentences begin with 'I' and focus on how this makes us feel.

The challenge for us when faced with a situation where we cannot clearly see a way to help is to focus on the other person.

Sometimes just by starting our sentences differently we change the focus.
'You are so important to me.'
'You are loved.'
'You are the centre of our thoughts and prayers.'
'You matter.'
By giving them these words, simple ones yet honestly spoken, we may help to rekindle a small flame.
And if we do not?

We do not have the power over darkness; that is the gift of God. We trust it will pass and we trust him to bring us into light again, for this is his dominion.
This is part of the tenet of our faith.

We must keep the flames burning in ourselves and in each other for this is one of the greatest gifts.

WE SHARE THE PEACE

Lord, let us come together as the family of Christ in your great light and sharing your peace.
Let us offer one another the sign of that peace.

SONG

'We'll walk the land with hearts on fire', *Mission Praise*, 743
'The Spirit lives to set us free', *Mission Praise*, 664
'God is light', *Hymns Ancient and Modern*, 364
'Beauty unspoken', *Songs of Fellowship*, 2222

WE PRAY TOGETHER

Let us pray.

Lord, as we come together tonight we offer you our prayers and confessions. We thank you for the gift of darkness, for the closing of the day, for the peace of the evening.
We praise you for the certainty of a new dawn, for the sureness that light will come again and that we will be reborn in you.

Lord, forgive us when we try to be all that we want to be in our own power, for when we fail to acknowledge you, for when we delight in our own achievements and become boastful.
Remind us, Lord, that our faith is strong thanks to your grace and that we are reflections of your holiness when we act in your name.
Amen.

Lord, as we contemplate the darkness that surrounds us now, help us to understand a little of what it means to feel that darkness inside.
Lord, in your mercy,
Hear our prayer.

Show us, Lord, those in our neighbourhoods, our communities, our families, who may be suffering their own internal darkness.
Lord, in your mercy,
Hear our prayer.

Open our eyes, Lord, to reveal the hidden pain that so many carry.
Lord, in our mercy,
Hear our prayer.

And, Lord, help us with humbleness and faith to reach out in small ways to those who need to see a little of your light.
Today, tomorrow and every day.
Lord, in your mercy,
Hear our prayer.

Lord, we thank you that you bring the day and the light.
And we thank you that the darkness reminds us of the dawn to come.
Amen.

Together we say the Lord's Prayer.
Our Father in heaven
Hallowed be your name.
Your kingdom come
Your will be done
On earth as it is in heaven.
Give us today our daily bread
And forgive us our trespasses
As we forgive those who trespass against us.
Lead us not into temptation
But deliver us from evil.
For the kingdom, the power and the glory are yours
Now and for ever.
Amen.

WE GO INTO THE WORLD TOGETHER

May you walk in the light and spread the flame of the word of God.
In the name of Christ.
Amen.

Spring

Burying the Alleluia

In this activity children decorate the letters of the word 'Alleluia' before burying them outside during Lent. They are then dug up and displayed for Easter.

Focus: Preparing for Easter through Lent.
Type of activity: Children's Sunday school activity.
Age range: 6 to 11 years.
Resources:
- Wallpaper lining paper or similar large sheets of paper, cardboard (e.g. from cardboard boxes), pencils, pens, paints, paint brushes, magazines containing pictures of things the children might like to thank God for, scissors and glue.
- A large air-tight box, plastic sheeting or bin bags.
- A spade and/or trowels.
- Somewhere outside to bury your Alleluia.
- A length of string or rope to display the Alleluia at Easter.

Aim

Many churches do not include 'Alleluias' in the liturgy throughout Lent as they move towards the most important festival in the church's year, Easter. Burying the Alleluia is an ancient tradition. You can use this activity with the children in your church to help them understand about preparing ourselves for Easter throughout Lent.

Structure

Creating your Alleluia
The outdoors bit
Displaying your Alleluia
An additional element

Creating your Alleluia

Towards the start of Lent make a set of large letters that spell out the word 'Alleluia'. The letters should be large and plain and quite chunky. Wallpaper lining paper is ideal; make letters more than 50cm tall. The letters will be coloured in by the children with pictures and words. Stick them to cardboard to make them more robust.

Alleluia means 'Praise the Lord', so talk to the children about what things they would like to celebrate – things that make them happy and that they would like to thank God for. They can then use these ideas to create pictures inside the letters to illustrate their own Alleluia. Use paint, coloured pens, collage, etc. to decorate the letters. You want to end up with each letter filled with pictures and words of celebration.

The outdoors bit

Talk to the children about why we give things up for Lent; say that it is a time to look at what we do and who we are, and that we are sorry for what we have done wrong and try to do better. To remind ourselves as a church that this is a time to say sorry we do a number of things: we dress the altar plainly and the clergy wear sombre colours; we do not have flowers on the altar; we sing songs about being sorry and we don't use the word 'Alleluia' in the services.

On the first Sunday in Lent the children literally 'bury the Alleluia'. Choose an air-tight container that won't leak and let water in, or wrap the letters up well in several layers of plastic sheeting or bin bags. You need to make sure your letters will not get damaged or go mouldy while they are underground. If you decide to do this every year, you might want to consider getting a special container in which to bury your Alleluia.

Go outside and walk around your church grounds with the children, looking for a suitable spot for burying your Alleluia. You will need to find somewhere that is not only big enough, but is easy to dig and will not be disturbed until you want to dig it up again. (You could choose a place in advance and also loosen the earth prior to the activity to make it easier for the children to dig.)

Let the children dig a hole in which to bury your container, then place it inside the hole and cover it up. You could sing a song as you stand around the site, such

The hole for the Alleluia

as a Taizé 'Kyrie eleison' ('Lord, have mercy'). Make sure the children wash their hands when you have finished.

Mark the place, or just make a note of where you have buried it, maybe even creating a map with the children of your grounds and marking the location on it. Alternatively take a photograph of the spot so that it is easy to find at the end of Lent.

Displaying your Alleluia

On Easter Day, all go outside to dig up your Alleluia. This is a time of praise, to shout that Christ is risen: 'Praise the Lord, Alleluia!' Why not sing a song such as:

Songs

'Allelu, allelu, allelu, alleluia, praise ye the Lord', *Hymns Old and New*,
    Complete Anglican Edition, 283
'Alleluia, alleluia give thanks to the risen Lord', *Mission Praise*, 30
'Alleluia', *Mission Praise*, 29

Bring the Alleluia inside. Punch a hole in the top of each letter, then run them along a string or rope so that the Alleluia can be hung up and displayed in church.

The Alleluia is displayed

An additional element

You could dig up the Alleluia before Easter Day and make a sepulchre. You might use an altar to do this. Make a container out of large sheets of card wrapped around your altar front. On these the children and adults write things they are sorry about. The Alleluia is hidden in the sepulchre, then taken out and hung up on Easter Day. (See colour photos of the hole for the Alleluia, the sepulchre, and the Alleluia displayed on the website.)

The sepulchre

Creating an Easter garden over Holy Week

For this activity you create an Easter garden that takes you through the whole of the story of the Passion. Or you can create just one of the scenes from the story, for example three crosses for Good Friday. Create your Easter garden within the grounds of your church.

Focus: The creation of an Easter garden that reflects your own local community in the run-up to Easter Day.

Type of activity: A series of activities run throughout Holy Week.

Age range: One or more specific groups within the church community. One group could do it all or a different group could get involved each day. The whole church community can join in the celebrations.

Resources: These will depend on the location of your parish. A selection of resources are given below but see Monday of Holy Week too.

- Items for making your crosses: pieces of wood or metal poles, or tree branches. Make sure you have something appropriate to fix them together with and a way of securing them in the ground.
- Stones and pebbles (if you will be gathering these in large quantities it is best to buy a supply from a garden centre or builder's merchant, so as to be considerate of your environment).
- Greenery (could be collected from your church grounds on the Monday, or later as you create your garden).
- String and rope.
- Trays with edges to contain water; dustbin lids are also suitable.
- Items to use to make a tomb:
  - Clothes lines or airers can be used as structures for your tomb.
  - Blankets, sheets, tarpaulins or rugs, ideally grey, brown or green.
  - Clothes pegs, bungie cords and other items to tie the structure together.
  - Large pieces of cardboard – unfolded boxes can be used to make larger sheets of card, which can then be cut to shape.
  - Branches and sections of foliage.

- Flowers and containers to put them in.
- Chalk, ropes or strips of cloth, sticks, pine cones, leaves, etc. (use them to make outlines for paths and spaces).
- Large sheets of paper (e.g. wallpaper lining paper), pencils and pens.
- A length of cloth to drape over your central cross and a white sheet for a grave cloth.

Aim

To create an Easter garden within your church's grounds that can be visited by the church community or opened up to the wider community.

Structure

Overview
Monday – Collect the elements of your garden together
Tuesday – Design your garden
Wednesday – Start preparing your garden
Maundy Thursday – Create the Garden of Gethsemane
Good Friday – Create Calvary
Saturday – The burial of Jesus
Sunday – Commemorating Easter Day

Overview

This series of activities over the week leads up to the creation of an Easter garden in your church's grounds. Each activity could take as little as an hour to complete (or much longer if you want to be really creative). If people cannot meet every day, all the activities could be undertaken on one day. Alternatively a different group could work on the garden each day.

Where you are located and the space you are using for your garden will affect what type of garden you can create. Here we describe some ideas for different features within a garden, but the whole point of this activity is to make something unique for your church and community. You could make it almost life-sized or in miniature, it really doesn't matter. (See colour photo of a miniature Easter garden on the website.)

If you do not have the time or capacity to work on this every day or build all the scenes, choose to make just one element to create, for example the three crosses.

Monday – Collect the elements of your garden together

This is the most important part of making your garden as it will define what your garden will look like.

Ask everyone in advance to bring different items to form part of your garden. You can give people some ideas as to what to choose; otherwise you could end up with a lot of unsuitable items you won't be able to use. See the list of resources above for ideas about what you will need.

A miniature Easter garden

You could make sure you collect all the different items you need, rather than lots of one thing, by writing ideas on cards and handing these out to the group and asking them to bring the items in. Be prepared to top up with anything that hasn't been allocated.

Discuss the various elements of your garden and decide which of the items you have collected will be used for each part of your garden. If you are representing the whole story the garden should contain at least the following:

- Three crosses.
- A tomb with a stone to roll over its entrance.
- Lots of flowers and green foliage making a garden area.

It could also contain:

- A pathway to the tomb.
- A pool of water for reflection.

At this stage you want to complete your planning as to how you will create the various elements of the garden with the materials you have gathered, and how they might fit together. Tomorrow you will decide how they will actually work in the space; right now you are planning how to make your crosses, how to build the tomb, etc. Also make a list of any extra things you need to collect for the construction of your garden or to improve its effect. For your crosses, for example, you may need to bring some means of tying the branches together. Or you might want to add in images or sculptures, poems or Bible verses.

Tuesday – Design your garden

If you have plenty of time in which to create your garden and want to involve as many members of the church community as possible, look at the information about how to design a space in 'Making your outside spaces the best they can be', in the final section of this book.

The following is a straightforward method that will, however, be sufficient for this activity.

Decide where in your grounds your garden is going to be located. You do not have to use just one space; for example, your crosses might be in one location and the tomb in another. It might be useful to include existing features into your garden, such as a pathway or trees.

Draw your final design on a sheet of paper. Include a description of how the different elements in your design will tell the story. You could include the relevant Bible verses (see below); these can be laminated and displayed by or in your garden so that visitors can see what you are doing. You could also write down and display the description of each stage as you develop the garden, and create pictures that can be displayed around your grounds telling the story of the run-up to Easter.

Wednesday – Start preparing your garden

Matthew 26.14–16
Judas arranges his betrayal of Jesus with the high priests

Then one of the Twelve – the one called Judas Iscariot – went to the chief priests and asked, 'What are you willing to give me if I deliver him over to you?' So they counted out for him thirty pieces of silver. From then on Judas watched for an opportunity to hand him over.

Use your plans to guide you on starting to create your garden outside. Mark out the pathways, areas and features. Use chalk on hard surfaces, strips of cloth or rope, or sticks, stones, pine cones, etc. to create your lines. On this first day of making the garden you are not being too specific here; rather you are marking out how all the different areas relate to each other outside in your grounds.

You can also start displaying around the site your descriptions of what is happening as you move towards Easter Sunday, so that others within your church community, or people passing by, can see what you are doing.

Maundy Thursday – Create the Garden of Gethsemane

Matthew 26.36–56
Gethsemane

Then Jesus went with his disciples to a place called Gethsemane, and he said to them, 'Sit here while I go over there and pray.' He took Peter and the two sons of Zebedee along with him, and he began to be sorrowful and troubled. Then he said to them, 'My soul is overwhelmed with sorrow to the point of death. Stay here and keep watch with me.'

Going a little farther, he fell with his face to the ground and prayed, 'My Father, if it is possible, may this cup be taken from me. Yet not as I will, but as you will.'

Then he returned to his disciples and found them sleeping. 'Couldn't you men keep watch with me for one hour?' he asked Peter. 'Watch and pray so that you will not fall into temptation. The spirit is willing, but the flesh is weak.'

He went away a second time and prayed, 'My Father, if it is not possible for this cup to be taken away unless I drink it, may your will be done.'

When he came back, he again found them sleeping, because their eyes were heavy. So he left them and went away once more and prayed the third time, saying the same thing.

Then he returned to the disciples and said to them, 'Are you still sleeping and resting? Look, the hour has come, and the Son of Man is delivered into the hands of sinners. Rise! Let us go! Here comes my betrayer!'

Jesus arrested

While he was still speaking, Judas, one of the Twelve, arrived. With him was a large crowd armed with swords and clubs, sent from the chief priests and the elders of the people. Now the betrayer had arranged a signal with them: 'The one I kiss is the man; arrest him.' Going at once to Jesus, Judas said, 'Greetings, Rabbi!' and kissed him.

Jesus replied, 'Do what you came for, friend.'

Then the men stepped forward, seized Jesus and arrested him. With that, one of Jesus' companions reached for his sword, drew it out and struck the servant of the high priest, cutting off his ear.

'Put your sword back in its place,' Jesus said to him, 'for all who draw the sword will die by the sword. Do you think I cannot call on my Father, and he will at once put at my disposal more than twelve legions of angels? But how then would the Scriptures be fulfilled that say it must happen in this way?'

In that hour Jesus said to the crowd, 'Am I leading a rebellion, that you have come out with swords and clubs to capture me? Every day I sat in the temple courts teaching, and you did not arrest me. But this has all taken place that the writings of the prophets might be fulfilled.' Then all the disciples deserted him and fled.

Today you are going to develop one specific space within your garden – the Garden of Gethsemane. This was where Jesus prayed, and his disciples slept, the day before he was crucified.

The aim here is to make a peaceful garden where people can sit to think about what is about to happen. Olive trees would have grown in the Garden of Gethsemane, so if you have trees in your grounds this could be a good location. Otherwise, use whatever you can to create your own trees: branches fixed into the ground or into buckets of sand or soil (as you would secure a Christmas tree), or make some trees out of cardboard.

Add other foliage and pots of flowers around the area – this is an opportunity to create a peaceful garden, a place for prayer and contemplation. You could add in water features, sculptures or other artworks to create the right atmosphere.

Good Friday – Create Calvary

Matthew 27.32–56
The crucifixion of Jesus

As they were going out, they met a man from Cyrene, named Simon, and they forced him to carry the cross. They came to a place called Golgotha (which means 'the place of the skull'). There they offered Jesus wine to drink, mixed with gall; but after tasting it, he refused to drink it. When they had crucified him, they divided up his clothes by casting lots. And sitting down, they kept watch over him there. Above his head they placed the written charge against him: THIS IS JESUS, THE KING OF THE JEWS.

Two rebels were crucified with him, one on his right and one on his left. Those who passed by hurled insults at him, shaking their heads and saying, 'You who are going to destroy the temple and build it in three days, save yourself! Come down from the cross, if you are the Son of God!' In the same way the chief priests, the teachers of the law and the elders mocked him. 'He saved others,' they said, 'but he can't save himself! He's the king of Israel! Let him come down now from the cross, and we will believe in him. He trusts in God. Let God rescue him now if he wants him, for he said, "I am the Son of God."' In the same way the rebels who were crucified with him also heaped insults on him.

The death of Jesus

From noon until three in the afternoon darkness came over all the land. About three in the afternoon Jesus cried out in a loud voice, 'Eli, Eli, lema sabachthani?' (which means 'My God, my God, why have you forsaken me?'). When some of those standing there heard this, they said, 'He's calling Elijah.'

Immediately one of them ran and got a sponge. He filled it with wine vinegar, put it on a staff, and offered it to Jesus to drink. The rest said, 'Now leave him alone. Let's see if Elijah comes to save him.'

And when Jesus had cried out again in a loud voice, he gave up his spirit.

At that moment the curtain of the temple was torn in two from top to bottom. The earth shook, the rocks split and the tombs broke open. The bodies of many holy people who had died were raised to life. They came out of the tombs after Jesus' resurrection and went into the holy city and appeared to many people.

When the centurion and those with him who were guarding Jesus saw the earthquake and all that had happened, they were terrified, and exclaimed, 'Surely he was the Son of God!'

Many women were there, watching from a distance. They had followed Jesus from Galilee to care for his needs. Among them were Mary Magdalene, Mary the mother of James and Joseph, and the mother of Zebedee's sons.

Today you will create the most significant part of your Easter garden – the three crosses.

Try to reflect your local area and community in the materials used in your crosses, making them have true meaning to your lives.

The crosses in the photograph are made from pine branches as this church is located within a pine wood. (See colour photo of crosses made from pine trees on the website.)

Crosses made from pine branches

You could add a crown of thorns to your central cross. Apart from this they should remain a stark reminder of the horrors of crucifixion and Jesus' death.

Saturday – The burial of Jesus

Matthew 27.57–61

As evening approached, there came a rich man from Arimathea, named Joseph, who had himself become a disciple of Jesus. Going to Pilate, he asked for Jesus' body, and Pilate ordered that it be given to him. Joseph took the body, wrapped it in a clean linen cloth, and placed it in his own new tomb that he had cut out of the rock. He rolled a big stone in front of the entrance to the tomb and went away. Mary Magdalene and the other Mary were sitting there opposite the tomb.

On this day we remember the burial of Jesus, so the task for the day is to make the tomb.

Build your tomb out of the materials you have gathered – rugs, tarpaulins, etc., – creating a space where a body could be laid inside. Add rocks and stones, branches and foliage around the outside to hide the structure. You can also add a flat stone where a body could be laid inside, perhaps using an existing bench or a row of boxes.

Finally make a stone to roll in front of your tomb – a large sheet of painted cardboard is ideal (it should last the few days of being outside). Whatever you use remember to make sure that it is easy to use and that no one can get hurt moving it.

Sunday – Commemorating Easter Day

Matthew 28.1–10
Jesus has risen

After the Sabbath, at dawn on the first day of the week, Mary Magdalene and the other Mary went to look at the tomb.

There was a violent earthquake, for an angel of the Lord came down from heaven and, going to the tomb, rolled back the stone and sat on it. His appearance was like lightning, and his clothes were white as snow. The guards were so afraid of him that they shook and became like dead men.

The angel said to the women, 'Do not be afraid, for I know that you are looking for Jesus, who was crucified. He is not here; he has risen, just as he said. Come and see the place where he lay. Then go quickly and tell his disciples: "He has risen from the dead and is going ahead of you into Galilee. There you will see him." Now I have told you.'

So the women hurried away from the tomb, afraid yet filled with joy, and ran to tell his disciples. Suddenly Jesus met them. 'Greetings,' he said. They came to him, clasped his feet and worshipped him. Then Jesus said to them, 'Do not be afraid. Go and tell my brothers to go to Galilee; there they will see me.'

Drape your central cross with a cloth and roll your gravestone away. Both these acts help us to remember the resurrection story. You could also leave a grave cloth in the tomb.

Now the garden is complete, you may wish to act out the story of Holy Week and Easter using the garden as the setting for the story.

Alternatively, you may want to encourage people just to walk through the story of Easter as they make their way through the garden. Displaying the story or Bible verses on a plan of the route or next to each feature will help them contemplate the sacrifice Jesus made and the wondrous story of Easter.

The living stones

SERVICE

Focus: Thinking about our concept of Church.
Resources:
- A selection of stones of varying sizes, one for every member of the congregation.
- Indelible marker pens.

WE GATHER FOR WORSHIP

Welcome, everyone, to this outdoor service.

Today we are thinking about what it means to be Church, as individuals and as a community both inward-looking and outward-facing.

As an expression of our faith and as a symbol of our love for God we will focus on understanding our role in our community and how we can strengthen our work in his name.

SONG

'Ascribe greatness to our God the rock', *Mission Praise*, 40
'Father, Lord of all creation', *Hymns Ancient and Modern*, 356
'Come, satisfy us', *Songs of Fellowship*, 2250

WE SAY SORRY

Our Lord and heavenly Father, we ask your forgiveness for being too inward-looking.
We know that you wish your Church to be a servant Church.

Lord, we pledge to focus more on the needs of others and the needs of the world around us and less on our own selfish and petty desires.

Lord, make our hearts bigger and more outward-looking, and help us to serve you by loving our neighbours better.

Lord, in your mercy,
Hear our prayer.

WE ARE FORGIVEN

Our Lord God, who is merciful and loves us his children, shows us the way of repentance and gives us strength to try harder and do better.

Our Lord God, who is merciful and loves us his children, gives us the tools that we need to right our wrongs and seek the better path.

Our Lord God, who is merciful and loves us his children, delights in our endeavours and takes great joy when we serve others more humbly.

WE AFFIRM OUR FAITH

We believe in one God,
the Father, the Almighty,
maker of heaven and earth,
of all that is, seen and unseen.

We believe in one Lord, Jesus Christ,
the only Son of God,
eternally begotten of the Father,
God from God, Light from Light,
true God from true God,
begotten, not made,
of one Being with the Father.
Through him all things were made.

For us and for our salvation
he came down from heaven:
by the power of the Holy Spirit
he became incarnate from the Virgin Mary,
and was made man.

For our sake he was crucified under Pontius Pilate;
he suffered death and was buried.
On the third day he rose again
in accordance with the Scriptures;
he ascended into heaven
and is seated at the right hand of the Father.
He will come again in glory to judge the living and the dead,
and his kingdom will have no end.

We believe in the Holy Spirit, the Lord, the giver of life,
who proceeds from the Father and the Son.
With the Father and the Son he is worshipped and glorified.
He has spoken through the Prophets.
We believe in one holy catholic and apostolic Church.
We acknowledge one baptism for the forgiveness of sins.
We look for the resurrection of the dead,
and the life of the world to come.
Amen.

SONG

'In the name of the Father', *Mission Praise*, 1192
'Tell out my soul', *Hymns Ancient and Modern*, 422
'Father of everlasting grace', *Songs of Fellowship*, 2273

READINGS

1 Peter 2.4–10
The living Stone and a chosen people
As you come to him, the living Stone – rejected by humans but chosen by God and precious to him – you also, like living stones, are being built into a spiritual house to be a holy priesthood, offering spiritual sacrifices acceptable to God through Jesus Christ. For in Scripture it says:
'See, I lay a stone in Zion,
    a chosen and precious cornerstone,
and the one who trusts in him
    will never be put to shame.'

Now to you who believe, this stone is precious. But to those who do not believe,
  'The stone the builders rejected
    has become the cornerstone,'
and,
  'A stone that causes people to stumble
    and a rock that makes them fall.'
They stumble because they disobey the message – which is also what they were destined for.

But you are a chosen people, a royal priesthood, a holy nation, God's special possession, that you may declare the praises of him who called you out of darkness into his wonderful light. Once you were not a people, but now you are the people of God; once you had not received mercy, but now you have received mercy.

1 Corinthians 3.10–14

By the grace God has given me, I laid a foundation as a wise builder, and someone else is building on it. But each one should build with care. For no one can lay any foundation other than the one already laid, which is Jesus Christ. If anyone builds on this foundation using gold, silver, costly stones, wood, hay or straw, their work will be shown for what it is, because the Day will bring it to light. It will be revealed with fire, and the fire will test the quality of each person's work. If what has been built survives, the builder will receive a reward.

TALK

I'd like you to think for a moment about our church, the building where we worship, the house of God that we attend every week.
What do you recall about its physical structure, but also about how it makes you feel?

Give the congregation a chance to respond either by talking among themselves or by sharing as part of the larger group.

Now I would like you to visualize in your mind how the church may be viewed by others in the community: maybe by new people moving in or those who have never set foot inside our building.

Again – give the congregation a chance to respond either by talking among themselves or by sharing as part of the larger group.

And now, what words would we want these people to use to describe the church that we know and love?

Invite all members of the congregation to take a stone and write their vision on the stone, placing them one by one to make a pile or a cairn, ideally somewhere in the grounds of the church where it can be revisited, or in front of the building where it can be seen by others. As they place the stone they speak the vision out loud.

When the cairn is built, repeat some of the words/visions that you can see or that you remember.

These words that you ascribe to the stones speak also of who we are and who God wants us to be. Each vision is not that of a building but of a people. You are the living stones and it is your faith and example that will draw others near to hear God's word.

We need our church building and it is important that we think about how it appears to others and that we do what we can to make it welcoming, but it is also important that we understand that *we* are church; it is *us* who must welcome and lead by example.

During the next week I invite you to allow thoughts of church to occur to you during your prayers – think about how we might fulfil the visions that you have described and make our church a place of honest worship and a living sacrifice to others.

By doing this we become Church during the week at home and at work as well as Church in this place at the weekend.

In a few months we will revisit this place and consider whether we have made any of the changes that we promised, and we will see if what we have built survives.

This covenant of stones will inspire us to create the church that we know we should offer our community.

WE SHARE THE PEACE

Lord, you give us great peace and we long to share that peace with others.
Let us share a sign of peace with one another now and by doing so commit to spreading that peace beyond the walls of our church.

SONG

'I will build my church', *Mission Praise*, 305
'Come, workers for the Lord', *Hymns Ancient and Modern*, 350
'You came to us the Servant King', *Songs of Fellowship*, 2675

WE PRAY TOGETHER

Lord, as we gather in this place help us to hear your vision for your Church. Free us, Lord, from the misconceptions that we may have and open our minds to a new vision for a loving and serving place of worship.
Lord, in your mercy,
Hear our prayer.

Refresh our hearts, Lord, and inspire in us a new commitment to being your people in the world. Show us how you would have us be in this place.
Help us, Lord, to be like living stones, a spiritual sacrifice and the centre of our communities. Help us to be strong and resilient and welcoming.
Lord, in your mercy,
Hear our prayer.

Lord, we are your Church, your living stones, your sacrifice and your promise. Show us your vision for Church; show us how you would have us change, and where we are doing what is good and pleasing in your sight.
Lord, in your mercy,
Hear our prayer.

Give us courage, Lord, to change our ways and challenge ourselves to look differently on our institution.
Reveal to us, we pray, Lord, the need in our community and how we might meet that need in your strength.
Lord, in your mercy,
Hear our prayer.

Together we say the Lord's Prayer.
Our Father in heaven
Hallowed be your name.
Your kingdom come
Your will be done
On earth as it is in heaven.
Give us today our daily bread
And forgive us our trespasses
As we forgive those who trespass against us.
Lead us not into temptation
But deliver us from evil.
For the kingdom, the power and the glory are yours
Now and for ever.
Amen.

WE GO INTO THE WORLD TOGETHER

Lord, as we go into your service now for the days ahead, strengthen and renew us and keep us inspired through your divine promise.

Keep our eyes facing heavenwards and prompt us to look to you when times are difficult and when things go wrong.

Remind us that our strength is in you alone.

Go in peace to love and serve the Lord.
In the name of Christ.
Amen.

Ascension Day kite flying

Flying kites to remember the story of Jesus' ascension.

Focus: The ascension.
Age range: 6 to 16 years, or the whole church working in intergenerational groups.
Type of activity: As part of an away day, a Sunday school activity or youth activity.
Resources:
- Kites.
- Small strips of paper and pens.
- Materials for adding decorations, such as tissue paper and glue.

Aim

To decorate and fly kites as an illustration of Jesus' ascension.

Structure

The Ascension Day story
Reading
The Bermudian tradition
Added extras
Flying your kites

The Ascension Day story

Talk about the story of the ascension and how it fits into the story of Jesus, before reading it from the Bible. Jesus appeared to his disciples after his crucifixion and resurrection, spoke to them about how the Holy Spirit would be sent to them, and then left them to be with his Father in heaven. From this time the disciples understood the Scriptures and were ready to spread the good news.

Reading

Luke 24.36–53
Jesus appears to the disciples
While they were still talking about this, Jesus himself stood among them and said to them, 'Peace be with you.'

They were startled and frightened, thinking they saw a ghost. He said to them, 'Why are you troubled, and why do doubts rise in your minds? Look at my hands and my feet. It is I myself! Touch me and see; a ghost does not have flesh and bones, as you see I have.'

When he had said this, he showed them his hands and feet. And while they still did not believe it because of joy and amazement, he asked them, 'Do you have anything here to eat?' They gave him a piece of broiled fish, and he took it and ate it in their presence.

He said to them, 'This is what I told you while I was still with you: everything must be fulfilled that is written about me in the Law of Moses, the Prophets and the Psalms.'

Then he opened their minds so they could understand the Scriptures. He told them, 'This is what is written: the Messiah will suffer and rise from the dead on the third day, and repentance for the forgiveness of sins will be preached in his name to all nations, beginning at Jerusalem. You are witnesses of these things. I am going to send you what my Father has promised; but stay in the city until you have been clothed with power from on high.'

The ascension of Jesus
When he had led them out to the vicinity of Bethany, he lifted up his hands and blessed them. While he was blessing them, he left them and was taken up into heaven. Then they worshipped him and returned to Jerusalem with great joy. And they stayed continually at the temple, praising God.

The Bermudian tradition

In Bermuda there is a tradition of flying kites on Good Friday afternoon. Wherever you are on the islands, you will see kites flying high above you in a multitude of colours. However, it is said that the original kite was flown by a teacher trying to find a simple way to demonstrate Christ's ascension, so that is why we are suggesting flying kites for this occasion.

There is a particular style of kite flown in Bermuda, although with several variations. They are quite tricky to make, though, so we suggest you buy ready-made ones of whatever type you like. However, you can find instructions for making traditional Bermuda kites online if you want to take this activity a step further.

Added extras

Whichever type of kite you choose, you can add extra features to give them more meaning:

- Add prayers or messages to the tail of the kite. Write your words on strips of paper and then attach them to the tail. These can symbolize your thoughts and prayers rising towards God. You could choose a theme for your messages – maybe focusing on the natural world around us.
- Decorate your kite, for example with the figure of Jesus – as the kite rises so he ascends.

At the end of the session it is important that there is plenty of time for everyone to fly their kites! Reflect on how we think of Jesus going up into heaven on Ascension Day, and this is why we are flying kites, but this also means that the Holy Spirit is always with us even though we can't see Jesus now.

You may want to link this with Pentecost activities, where the wind is connected with the action of the Holy Spirit.

Pentecost wind and fire

A range of simple activities that can be done separately over a number of sessions or all together in one day. Activities focus on wind and fire as representations of the Holy Spirit at Pentecost.

Focus: The coming of the Holy Spirit at Pentecost.
Type of activity: Activities for a family activity day. Alternatively, individual activities can be used in a children's group.
Age range: All ages – including children and parents and carers.
Resources:
- Badges/labels, coloured pens.
- If you do all the activities you will need:
  - Large sheets of thick card (approximately 1m by 1m).
  - One or more kite(s).
  - Squares of paper (20cm by 20cm), dowels, drawing pins or other flat-ended pin.
  - Long ribbons, glue.
  - Card (10cm by 25cm), paper clips.
  - A camp fire, or barbecue and fuel. See separate activities below for things to cook.
  - Large candles, tapers or lanterns and matches.

Aim

The aim of the day is to think about what the first Pentecost was like. By experiencing fire and wind, participants gain an understanding of how the early apostles felt.

The writer of Acts describes the experience of the Holy Spirit at the first Pentecost as being like wind and fire. Both of these are best experienced outside and a range of different ways of doing this are put together here into a day of activities.

Children and families are encouraged to think about what the first Pentecost might have been like. Alternatively, pick out one or two activities to undertake during a shorter session.

Structure of a day

10am: Gathering and welcome
10.15am: Reading and discussion
10.30am: Feeling the wind
11.20am: Break – make a hot drink over the camp fire
11.40am: Continue more wind activities
12.30pm: Lunch around a fire
1.30pm: The effect of fire
2pm: Bringing it all together
3pm: Finish

Gathering and welcome

Make sure you register participants on the day so that you know who you are responsible for and that everyone is accounted for throughout the day. Adults and children alike should be given a badge or label on which they write their names. They can also decorate them, perhaps using the theme of wind and fire within their decorations.

When everyone is gathered together, talk about keeping safe when working with fire. See the health and safety section of this book about undertaking a risk-benefit assessment and working safely with fire.

Explain the structure of the day.

Reading and discussion

Acts 2.1–4
The Holy Spirit comes at Pentecost
When the day of Pentecost came, they were all together in one place. Suddenly a sound like the blowing of a violent wind came from heaven and filled the whole house where they were sitting. They saw what seemed to be tongues of

fire that separated and came to rest on each of them. All of them were filled with the Holy Spirit and began to speak in other tongues as the Spirit enabled them.

Discussion questions to ask children in particular

- The Apostles described the Holy Spirit as sounding like a rushing wind. Have you ever been somewhere indoors where you can really hear the wind outside? What did that sound like?
- 'The sound then filled the whole house.' How would you feel if you thought a really strong wind blowing outside might suddenly come into your house? What might happen if it did?

Feeling the wind

Like the Holy Spirit, you cannot see the wind and you cannot touch it, but you can see its impact. So finding different ways to experience the wind can be a useful way to explain the impact of the Holy Spirit.

Set up a series of activities that show the impact of the wind (see below). With a small group you can run these one after the other; with a large group you can set up stations where the different activities take place with small groups, and people rotate around the activities.

Select your activities and arrange each to last about 20–30 minutes (have a spare activity up your sleeve, in case one of them finishes sooner than expected and you have a gap to fill). If everyone completes each activity they will all have had a go at experiencing the wind in all available ways. Do not stress the link to the Holy Spirit at this stage – let everyone get involved in the activities and experience the impact of the wind.

Suggested activities

- Take it in turns to run with a large sheet of card held in front of you. Even on a calm day you can feel the impact of the wind as you run. (This is a short activity so it could be combined with one of the others.)
- Fly a kite. Make sure everyone has a go at holding the strings and feeling the power of the wind on the kite.

- Make windmills. These are simple to make using a 20cm square of paper, a dowel and a drawing pin. The sails can be made to move by blowing. Take the square of paper and cut in towards the centre from the corners, leaving about 5cm uncut in the middle. Fold the alternate corners into the centre of the square and fix to the dowel with your drawing pin. Make sure that the sails are free to rotate. You can decorate your windmills and also make them in different sizes (see illustration).

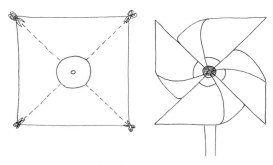

Making a windmill

- Streamers can be made using dowels and long ribbons of varying widths – 2cm to 10cm, and at least 2m long. Tie the ribbon around one end of the stick and glue it in place. Once you have made your streamer run around with it held out behind you or create shapes by trailing the streamer in the air. (See colour photo of a riband on the website.)

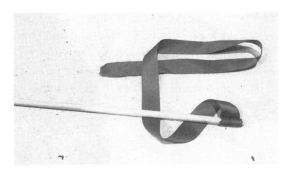

A riband

- Helicopters made of stiff paper or card are great to use from a height. On a 10cm by 25cm strip of card, make a slit to just less than halfway down the centre lengthways. Then, leaving about 2cm, make two slits across the centre of the card to about a third of the way in from each side. Fold these two sections over so that the base is now a third the width of the top. Fold up about 1cm of the bottom of the card/paper and secure with a paper clip. Then fold down the two sections at the top, one each way, so that they are horizontal. Now drop this helicopter from a height and see it spin in the air, giving another example

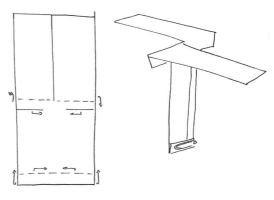

Making a helicopter

of the wind having an impact even though it can't be seen (see illustration).

- At the right time of year you can collect natural helicopters: ash keys or maple seeds are the natural version of the paper helicopter described above.
- Visit a wood or the sea where you can see the wind in action.
- Discuss situations where you can see the effect of the wind.

Lunch

Have your lunch around a camp fire or barbecue (see the section on health and safety).

At Pentecost believers came together and shared all they had. Why not have a bring-and-share barbecue so that everyone can get together as a family?

Ideas of what to cook over a camp fire or barbecue include:

- **Pancakes.** These are easy and quick to cook on a pan over the fire.

- **Bannock bread.** This is made using a simple dough. You can cook them over the fire on the end of a stick. Whittle the bark off sticks the thickness of a finger and wrap strips of dough around them in a spiral. Hold them over the glowing embers, turning your stick until the dough is cooked evenly. Alternatively, make small flat cakes and cook them on a tray or skillet. (See colour photo of cooking bread (and vegetarian sausages) on the website.)

Cooking bread and vegetarian sausages

Here is one recipe for Bannock bread – there are other variants.

3 cups flour
1 tsp baking powder
1 tsp salt
½ cup dry milk powder
1 cup water

Mix the ingredients together well in a bowl. Divide the dough into a number of flattened loaves or rolls and cook these over your fire on a baking tray or in a pan.

Optional extras: sweet – raisins, or add jam when cooked; savoury – garlic or other herbs, or add butter when cooked.

- **Bananas with chocolate buttons.** Make a slit down the length of a banana, then place about six buttons inside. Use a square of foil to wrap up the banana completely. Use tongs to place the bananas in the embers of the fire. Cook for about 15 minutes, turning over halfway through. Unwrap and eat, very carefully scooping out the melted chocolate and cooked

Barbecuing bananas

banana with a teaspoon. The foil cools quickly but the fruit will be very hot so supervise younger children closely. (See colour photo of barbecuing bananas on the website.)

- **Hot chocolate.** It is easy to cook in a large pan over the fire. (See colour photo of cooking hot chocolate over a fire on the website.)

- **Toasting marshmallows on sticks.** Use long sticks (at least 50cm) so that children can keep a safe distance from the fire. They should kneel down near the fire to make sure they have a stable base. Some people prefer to set fire to the marshmallow, others like to hold them over glowing coals rather than in the flames, turning them as they become golden brown. Remind everyone that the marshmallows will be very hot, so they must wait for them to cool down before eating them. You can also place marshmallows between two chocolate biscuits to eat them – messy, but tasty.

The effect of fire

Fire is transformative, so any activity where fire changes something will help you explain how the Holy Spirit is like fire. It can change the ordinary into something even better.

- Making popcorn over a camp fire or barbecue shows how the heat of the fire changes what looks quite ordinary into something much more appealing. Use a heavy-based metal pot with a lid and add a little melted butter and oil. Place your popping corn inside, put the lid on and wait for the corn to pop. Give it an occasional shake. When the popping has stopped, remove from the fire and tip into a bowl. Add your own seasoning to taste.
- Talk about how fire is used to refine things, such as purifying metal. By heating a substance that is a mix of different chemicals, something can be extracted that is pure, beautiful and often valuable.
- Pentecost is often seen as the birth of the Church, so why not light some birthday candles? Take this idea outside and you can make them bigger and brighter. Use outdoor candles or tapers available from household goods shops, or buy or make lanterns and hold your service outside.

Bringing it all together

Sit around the fire and discuss what you have experienced over the day.

- How did you know that the wind was there? You saw and felt its impact but couldn't see it. How is this like the Holy Spirit?
- The apostles described their experience of the coming of the Holy Spirit as being like tongues of flame coming to rest on them. What do you think that might have been like?
- What kind of things do you think fire does that might be like the Holy Spirit? Ideas might include cleansing, lightening/brightening people up, providing energy.
- What impact did the coming of the Holy Spirit have on the apostles? What impact can the Holy Spirit have on our lives today?

Songs around the fire

'Spirit of the living God', *Mission Praise*, 613
'Breathe on me, breath of God', *Hymns Old and New*, Complete Anglican Edition, 85
'This little light of mine, I'm going to let it shine', Joel Rainey

A new creation

SERVICE

Focus: Using visual images of spring to remind us of God's great creation and our role in it.

Resources:

- Ideally use an outdoor space that has some visual clues of spring, such as spring bulbs in flower. You can plan ahead for this by planting bulbs in the autumn before.
- Encourage people to bring cameras, on phones or tablets or more traditional devices.

WE GATHER FOR WORSHIP

Welcome to this spring service!

We have come outside today to become more involved with the natural world that heralds our seasons and to remind ourselves of God's awesome creation.

SONG

'I am a new creation', *Mission Praise*, 254
'Nature with open volume', *Hymns Ancient and Modern*, 497
'Creation sings the Father's song', *Songs of Fellowship*, 2255

WE SAY SORRY

Lord, we are your children and your creation and in you we see our birth.

We ask your forgiveness, Lord, for straying from the life that you would have us live and for making choices that are not of your desiring.

Help us, Lord, we pray, to be a living reflection of you and of your son Jesus Christ and to turn from sin and embrace your glory.

WE ARE FORGIVEN

Our Lord God, who is mightier than mountains and more powerful than the strongest storm, has mercy on us, his children.

Our Lord God, who could cast us out into darkness, accepts our repentance and gives us new life in him.

Our Lord God loves us, whom he created in the image of his son, and wishes only that we try again and try harder.

Thank you, Father, for forgiving us.
Help us, we pray, to make our repentance true and lasting and righteous.

WE AFFIRM OUR FAITH

We believe in one God,
the Father, the Almighty,
maker of heaven and earth,
of all that is, seen and unseen.

We believe in one Lord, Jesus Christ,
the only Son of God,
eternally begotten of the Father,
God from God, Light from Light,
true God from true God,
begotten, not made,
of one Being with the Father.
Through him all things were made.

For us and for our salvation
he came down from heaven:
by the power of the Holy Spirit
he became incarnate from the Virgin Mary,
and was made man.

For our sake he was crucified under Pontius Pilate;
he suffered death and was buried.
On the third day he rose again
in accordance with the Scriptures;
he ascended into heaven
and is seated at the right hand of the Father.

He will come again in glory to judge the living and the dead,
and his kingdom will have no end.

We believe in the Holy Spirit, the Lord, the giver of life,
who proceeds from the Father and the Son.
With the Father and the Son he is worshipped and glorified.
He has spoken through the Prophets.
We believe in one holy catholic and apostolic Church.
We acknowledge one baptism for the forgiveness of sins.
We look for the resurrection of the dead,
and the life of the world to come.
Amen.

SONG

'All creatures of our God and King', *Mission Praise*, 7
'Help us to help each other', *Hymns Ancient and Modern*, 374
'At your name the mountains shake and tremble', *Songs of Fellowship*, 2220

READINGS

Song of Songs 2.11–12
> See! The winter is past;
>> the rains are over and gone.
> Flowers appear on the earth;
>> the season of singing has come,
> the cooing of doves
>> is heard in our land.

Genesis 1.11–14
> Then God said, 'Let the land produce vegetation: seed-bearing plants and trees on the land that bear fruit with seed in it, according to their various kinds.' And it was so. The land produced vegetation: plants bearing seed according

to their kinds and trees bearing fruit with seed in it according to their kinds. And God saw that it was good. And there was evening, and there was morning – the third day.

And God said, 'Let there be lights in the vault of the sky to separate the day from the night, and let them serve as signs to mark sacred times, and days and years.

TALK

How often do we think to ourselves: 'Where did the year go – is it really April/May/June already?'

How often do we see the months rushing past us with a sense of urgency and feel somehow left behind in the aftermath of time?

In these days of indoor activities, social media, long working hours and busy lives we often do not get the sense of the seasons rolling past with their slow but steady progress. Everything is rushed.

Month after month, small miracles are being worked all around us. Moments of utter perfection happen, hidden to our view.

Take a moment now to look around you with new eyes.

Focus only on that which is natural, on that which is a reminder of spring for you – of God's creation.

Take a moment to point out to each other, and to me, what those things are.

Give people a while to notice shoots coming through the soil, leaf buds on trees, blossom forming, the brightness of the sky and the smell of warm earth. They may hear the birdsong and even notice small mammals, depending on where you are holding your service.

Now I want you to take a closer look – move right in and notice what you are seeing.
A myriad of perfect creations, a myriad of new births.
Tiny, tiny plants and flowers that all grow one by one in their own way. Look at how delicate they are and yet how they survive in this world.
Every one of these is as well known to our Father God as we are.
Every one is as precious to him as we are, and look how perfect he made them.

Now take a picture of what you can see – get as close as you can and see the veins of the leaves, the colour of the shoots, the richness of the flowers.

How often, if ever, do we take the time to admire and respect God's creation in this way?

Even in this land that we have ruptured with our own less beautiful creations – still our Lord reigns.

Even in this land that we have hurt, whose resources we have wasted, still our Lord reigns.

Even in this land that we plunder remorselessly and throw away, still our Lord reigns.

If we were gone tomorrow, God's creation would survive. The natural world would take over as surely as the dandelion grows between the paving stones and will not be crushed.

If nature were gone tomorrow we would not last a week.

Look again at your photograph and marvel at the wonder of it.

I challenge all of you to use that image on your PCs and laptops, on your walls and on your fridge doors, to remind yourself of the power of what the Lord made. We too are his creation – and we too will overcome hardship and survive in times of darkness.

And we too are precious in his sight.

WE SHARE THE PEACE

Lord, as we stand with you and each other alongside your natural world, we marvel in your creation. Let us share the peace with one another as the wind blows and the sun shines on our worship.

SONG

'Oh breath of life', *Mission Praise*, 488
'For the fruits', *Hymns Ancient and Modern*, 457
'I see your face in every sunrise', *Songs of Fellowship*, 2372

WE PRAY TOGETHER

Lord, we gather today in your garden to thank you for our world.

Father, you entrust us with your precious kingdom here on earth and yet we do not cherish it as we should.

Show us your creation today, Lord, with new eyes. Instil in us the awe and wonder of nature and of every perfect and beautiful new birth.

As your word comes to life after the cold winter, revive us also here in your church.
In Jesus' name.
Amen.

Lord, thank you that we are as precious to you as the flower, the tree, the dove.

That you created us all.

Lord, in this time of a new spring, of rebirth, may we also be reborn in you as children of your creation.

Remind us daily, Lord, that we are just guardians of your world and that we must work harder to fulfil this duty.

Show us, Lord, how to care.

In Jesus' name.
Amen.

**Our Father in heaven
Hallowed be your name.
Your kingdom come
Your will be done
On earth as it is in heaven.
Give us today our daily bread
And forgive us our trespasses
As we forgive those who trespass against us.
Lead us not into temptation
But deliver us from evil.
For the kingdom, the power and the glory are yours
Now and for ever.
Amen.**

WE GO INTO THE WORLD TOGETHER

So go out into the world today with a new blessing in your heart, the warmth of the sun on your back and the knowledge of God's lovingkindness.

You are all truly wonders of his creation.

Rogation, beating the bounds

An activity for the whole church community. It involves walking between churches, or around your parish boundary or other route, and can finish with a picnic.

Focus: Rogation.
Type of activity: Whole church activity.
Age range: The whole church community can join in the celebrations.
Resources:
* A map of your parish boundary, or the route you are using to travel on.
* Resources for a picnic – food, drink, rugs, seats, etc.

Structure

What is beating the bounds?
The outdoors bit
   Beating the bounds activity
   Prayers for your journey

What is beating the bounds?

Rogation comes from the Latin *rogare* – 'to ask' – in this case asking for a blessing for the fields. Over the centuries it came to include the tradition of 'beating the bounds'. This involved processing around the parish boundaries where boys would be 'reminded' of the extent of the parish in a range of ways, including being held upside down and having their heads knocked on boundary stones, being rolled in the brambles, or being thrown into a pond. You may wish not to undertake these aspects of the tradition(!) but a procession along your boundary, between churches within a benefice, or between two churches that have, or would like to have, close connections, is a great way to mark this event in the church year.

It can be easy to see the relevance of blessing the fruits of the field in a rural parish, where the focus is on growing crops and on caring for young livestock, but a little more difficult in urban areas. So you might like to focus on other 'fruits' produced in your area, in gardens, parks and other open spaces, urban farms or other food producers. You could even extend the idea of fruits to other types of items produced in your area – manufactured products or the produce of the service industries.

The outdoors bit

Beating the bounds activity

Beating the bounds in Waterloo, London

Beating the bounds is a great occasion to bring your church together, and also means that you get to see more of your parish.

The main part of the activity is a walk. Traditionally this should be around the boundary of your parish, but could be between two or more churches, or between various important places, perhaps starting or finishing at your church.

As you go along your journey, in the countryside stop along the way to bless the crops as you pass by. In urban areas you could plan your journey to go past places that are important in other ways within your own community.

You could end your walk at a particular place or space for a picnic together. Encourage people of all ages to join you. Make it a real church family occasion. Invite people to bring dogs with them on the journey.

Include the less mobile members of your church by making sure that they can be part of the journey activity. This might be by transporting them along the route in some way or arranging to meet them at the destination.

Prayers for your journey

Crops

Lord, we thank you for the gifts of food from your creation. We pray for the farmers and those who fill our tables with our daily bread, and we offer to your care those in this world who do not have enough to eat.

Lord, we thank you for the rains and the sun, for the earth and for the wind, and for all the parts of your creation that make this rich harvest.

Homes

Lord, you give us shelter from the world and space to be with our families. We ask you to bless these homes and those that live within them.

We praise you and thank you for the gift of family life. Lord, we offer to you those who are alone and lonely at this time, and pray for those who feel unsafe or frightened in their homes. Bless them and be near them, Lord.

Other places of worship

Father, we are all equal in your sight and you alone know our hearts. We pray for all those who worship, and for all those who cannot find it in their hearts to worship.

Bless our brothers and sisters, those who think and believe as we do and those who think and believe differently, for we are all one in your sight.

Shopping centres

Lord, we ask you to bless this place of commerce. We pray for the lives of those who trade goods and who make our lives more comfortable. We pray, Lord, for those who cannot afford the things that make our lives so comfortable, and we ask your blessing on those who succumb to temptation to take that which does not belong to them.

Police stations and courts

Lord, we bless the law-makers. May they be wise and exercise justice. Father, your word is our law above all others, but you make for us a pattern on earth that we must follow.

Father, guide those who seek to maintain order and keep us from harm. Bless and protect them and their families. Be with them as they go into danger, and guard them from evil.

Factories

Lord, bless the workers in this place. Guide them daily, and give those in authority over them grace and wisdom.

May the work of their hands be pleasing to you, Lord, and may they take pride in their toil. As they tire, give them renewed strength; as they face challenges, guide them. When they come home from their labours, bring them rest.

Summer

The lilies of the field

SERVICE

Focus: Using the Bible and God's word for reassurance in times of anxiety.
Resources:
- A small fire pit laid to light – choose one that stands slightly elevated from the ground, if you are not able to build one in your grounds.
- Paper and pens, given out to everyone.
- Matches.

WE GATHER FOR WORSHIP

Welcome today to this outdoor service where we will be giving thanks for our Lord's care of us.

Often we need to be reminded of his presence in our lives. It is the times when we forget this that hope can become far away and the pressure of living in today's world can feel like too much.

SONG

'The earth is the Lord's', *Mission Praise*, 642
'Christ is the heavenly food that gives', *Hymns Ancient and Modern*, 439
'Bless the Lord, O my soul', *Songs of Fellowship*, 2231

WE SAY SORRY

Lord, forgive us when we fail to lean on you but become over-burdened with cares and worries.

Forgive us when we fall on earthly solutions to our problems, and help us to learn to look to you.

Forgive us, Lord, that we hurt you when, as your children, we seek counsel elsewhere.

Forgive us, Lord, for forgetting to ask for and to receive your help.

WE ARE FORGIVEN

The Lord God who made us knows our weaknesses and forgives them when we truly repent.

He carries us in his heart and wishes nothing but our happiness and our comfort.

Our Lord God watches over us always and is quick to absolve us and free us from our sin.

WE AFFIRM OUR FAITH

We believe in one God,
the Father, the Almighty,
maker of heaven and earth,
of all that is, seen and unseen.

We believe in one Lord, Jesus Christ,
the only Son of God,
eternally begotten of the Father,
God from God, Light from Light,
true God from true God,
begotten, not made,
of one Being with the Father.
Through him all things were made.

For us and for our salvation
he came down from heaven:
by the power of the Holy Spirit
he became incarnate from the Virgin Mary,
and was made man.

For our sake he was crucified under Pontius Pilate;
he suffered death and was buried.
On the third day he rose again
in accordance with the Scriptures;
he ascended into heaven
and is seated at the right hand of the Father.

He will come again in glory to judge the living and the dead,
and his kingdom will have no end.

We believe in the Holy Spirit, the Lord, the giver of life,
who proceeds from the Father and the Son.
With the Father and the Son he is worshipped and glorified.
He has spoken through the Prophets.
We believe in one holy catholic and apostolic Church.
We acknowledge one baptism for the forgiveness of sins.
We look for the resurrection of the dead,
and the life of the world to come.
Amen.

SONG

'What a friend we have in Jesus', *Mission Praise*, 746
'Have faith in God, my heart', *Hymns Ancient and Modern*, 372
'Come to me all you who are weary', *Songs of Fellowship*, 2252

READINGS

Matthew 6.25–32
   Do not worry
   'Therefore I tell you, do not worry about your life, what you will eat or drink;
   or about your body, what you will wear. Is not life more than food, and the
   body more than clothes? Look at the birds of the air; they do not sow or reap

or store away in barns, and yet your heavenly Father feeds them. Are you not much more valuable than they? Can any one of you by worrying add a single hour to your life?

'And why do you worry about clothes? See how the flowers of the field grow. They do not labour or spin. Yet I tell you that not even Solomon in all his splendour was dressed like one of these. If that is how God clothes the grass of the field, which is here today and tomorrow is thrown into the fire, will he not much more clothe you – you of little faith? So do not worry, saying, "What shall we eat?" or "What shall we drink?" or "What shall we wear?" For the pagans run after all these things, and your heavenly Father knows that you need them.'

Psalm 1.1–3

Blessed is the one
    who does not walk in step with the wicked
or stand in the way that sinners take
    or sit in the company of mockers,
but whose delight is in the law of the Lord,
    and who meditates on his law day and night.
That person is like a tree planted by streams of water,
    which yields its fruit in season
and whose leaf does not wither –
    whatever they do prospers.

TALK

The whole difference between construction and creation is exactly this: that a thing constructed can only be loved after it is constructed; but a thing created is loved before it exists.

There are dark shadows on earth but its lights are stronger in the contrast.

No one is useless in this world who lightens the burden of it to anyone else.
(Charles Dickens)

Does anyone know who wrote the beautiful words in these three quotations?

Invite the congregation to make some guesses; someone of course may know.

These words for me are more than just beautiful words; they are deeply reassuring, they speak to our soul and provide it with comfort.

They are a reminder of God here today, right now, in every place and in every situation.

They are a reminder that God is as relevant to me and to my modern-day troubles and strifes now as he was in the days of David – or indeed Dickens.

They are a reminder that God has never let me down and he won't start now, however great the challenge, however complex the problem, however I think to myself, 'This is one that God can't handle so I won't bother praying on it,' or even worse – when it just does not cross my mind to ask God for help at all.

These words by Dickens are living proof of how God's comfort was relevant then; it is still as relevant now – he understands everything that we are going through.

When we reflect on the comforting words in Matthew we are reminded that God does indeed care for our every need.

Whether we are the birds of the air or the lilies of the field, he ensures that we have what we need – right here and right now.

We may worry about what we will have tomorrow, but that is not our concern, for God is in us today.

I'd like you to take a moment to think back to the last time (and it may even be right now) when you faced a problem, when you had that pit-of-the-stomach dropping feeling, when your heart began to race as you realized a situation was rapidly getting beyond your control.

What was your first response?
Did you begin to plan your way out of the mess?
Did you throw money at the problem?
Did you shout at a colleague?
Did you pick up the phone to someone who you thought could help?
Did you run to your manager or your partner for help?

Or did you pray?

Remember honestly what you did, and then share this with someone near you.

Allow a few moments for this to happen.

Many of us experience worries and anxiety every day, indeed, increasing numbers of people are being prescribed medication for stress, worry and anxiety.

And yet this is not how God wants us to live. He does not want us to struggle in this way.

He wants us to come to him in prayer and faithfulness.

The problem is often that if prayer is not ingrained in our habits, if we do not regularly take our problems to God, if our default is not to come to him, then in our times of panic we will not think to do so and we will rely on our own strength and power to save us.

We need to build this good habit, so that when faced with problems he is our first port of call, our first mentor.

And even just by reflecting our situation to him and allowing his Spirit to dwell on it, we will see the problem ahead in a new light. And we are not alone in it.

We may think that God cannot manage the challenges of the modern world; we may think that some problems are too personal, too uncomfortable, too bad for him to deal with.

We are wrong.

He has never let us down and he won't start now.

This is a good time to light the fire.

Take your piece of paper and, reflecting on a current problem, write a few words that describe your situation.

We will use the fire as a visual image to help remind you in the days and weeks and months to come.

Now place your paper in the fire and offer your problem to God in your heart.

Watch as the smoke rises. For many people the use of incense is a powerful visual reminder of our prayers going up to God, and this can be a useful tool. Maybe remember the smell of the fire today, the image of the smoke rising into the sky and disappearing, the act of writing the words on the paper and the sensation of leaving this one to God to reflect on for a while.

Commit these sensory memories to your heart in order that when again you are troubled, you remember first to come to God.

He has never let you down and he won't start now.

The whole difference between construction and creation is exactly this: that a thing constructed can only be loved after it is constructed; but a thing created is loved before it exists.

There are dark shadows on earth but its lights are stronger in the contrast.

No one is useless in this world who lightens the burden of it to anyone else.

WE SHARE THE PEACE

Let us come together as God's Church and share with one another the sign of the peace.

SONG

'Our God he lives forever', *Mission Praise*, 1347
'We find thee, Lord, in others' need', *Hymns Ancient and Modern*, 430
'Can you hear there's a new song', *Songs of Fellowship*, 2243

WE PRAY TOGETHER

Lord, we ask you to be with us today as we come together to reflect on your kindness and mercy.

As we consider your great goodness, help us to release to you any concerns or worries that might be weighing us down.
Lord, in your mercy,
Hear our prayer.

As we hold onto our troubles, take us by the hand and lead us to a quieter place where we might lay our burdens at your feet and ask for your wisdom.
Lord, in your mercy,
Hear our prayer.

Lord, you are here in our everyday, waiting and quietly watching.
We know you hurt, Father, when we refuse to ask you for help.
When we soldier on in our own power.
When we make worse the very situations that we seek to resolve.

Lord, be at our shoulder and remind us that you are there for us.
That you take our worries and our anxieties and acknowledge them and help us to make sense of them.
Lord, in your mercy,
Hear our prayer.

Thank you, Lord, that you have never let us down and you won't start now.
In Jesus' name.
Amen.

Our Father in heaven
Hallowed be your name.
Your kingdom come
Your will be done
On earth as it is in heaven.
Give us today our daily bread
And forgive us our trespasses
As we forgive those who trespass against us.
Lead us not into temptation
But deliver us from evil.
For the kingdom, the power and the glory are yours
Now and for ever.
Amen.

WE GO OUT INTO THE WORLD TOGETHER

Lord, as you send us out into the world, stay with us always.
Remind us daily of your grace and mercy and your love for us that cannot be consumed by any worry or anxiety, however overwhelming.
Walk with us, Lord, we pray in your mercy.
Amen.

A fish breakfast

Start a day away together or a church retreat by cooking and sharing a fish breakfast, just as Jesus shared with his disciples when he appeared to them after his crucifixion and resurrection.

Focus: Sharing a meal, in particular a meal that Jesus shared with his disciples. Based around John 21.1–14.
Type of activity: An early-morning activity at the start of an away day or the morning of a church retreat.
Age range: Either adults or the whole church community.
Resources:
- Mini barbecues – one for every five people.
- Fish, lemons, a vegetarian option, herbs, salt and pepper, bread, foil, plates, knives and forks.
- Water, first aid kit, barbecue tongs, fish slice.
- Sharp knives to gut and prepare the fish, chopping boards.
- Juice or lemonade to go with your fish breakfast.
- Bread and butter.
- 153 cardboard or paper fish, and some string bags or similar.

Aim

To bring members of your church community together at the start of a day away together; to share in an experience that the disciples shared with Jesus.

Structure

Preparing the fire and the fish (including an activity for younger children)
Cooking and sharing the fish

Preparing the fire and the fish

If you are involving younger children you may want to plan an activity to occupy them while you are preparing the fish. Make 153 cardboard fish and hide them around the area. Split the children into groups and give each group a net to collect the fish in (a string bag would be perfect) and set them off to find the fish. Make sure this takes place well away from the fires. If you use line drawings of your fish the children can colour these in later. Alternatively you can make some of them really bright so they are easy to find, and some in duller colours that are more camouflaged and take longer to find.

The older children and/or adults should prepare the fish and the fire.

- Light the mini barbecues about 30 minutes ahead of time to give them enough time to burn down to embers ready for cooking the fish (see the health and safety section about working with fire).
- You will need one barbecue between about every five people in order to cook all the fish you need at the same time.

Jobs that need to be done before cooking can begin include:

- Gutting and cleaning the fish.
- Preparing herbs and lemon slices to be cooked with the fish.
- Preparing squares of foil to wrap the fish in.
- Preparing bread to be eaten with the fish.
- Setting out the seating area around the fire – use picnic rugs and seats and tables for those who would prefer to sit this way. Make sure that everyone will be comfortable.
- Preparing drinks, cutlery and plates.
- Preparing a vegetarian option – a foil parcel of vegetables with oil and herbs is a good alternative. If you have plenty of vegetables these could also supplement your fish meal.

Cooking and sharing the fish

- Cooking takes place in small groups. Let the children join in with this if they want to, so that you all cook together.
- Each group collects their fish, herbs, lemon and foil, as well as bread and vegetables.
- Wrap the fish in squares of foil, adding the slices of lemon and herbs in and around the fish.

- Cook the fish on the barbecue grill, turning the parcels occasionally.
- You can also toast the bread over the barbecue.

In each group create your own grace for your meal before sharing and eating together.

As people eat, you can read through the passage and they can imagine what it must have been like to share food with someone you never expected to see again. How can you make this a special event and something you will always remember?

John 21.1–14

Afterwards Jesus appeared again to his disciples, by the Sea of Galilee. It happened this way: Simon Peter, Thomas (also known as Didymus), Nathanael from Cana in Galilee, the sons of Zebedee, and two other disciples were together. 'I'm going out to fish,' Simon Peter told them, and they said, 'We'll go with you.' So they went out and got into the boat, but that night they caught nothing.

Early in the morning, Jesus stood on the shore, but the disciples did not realize that it was Jesus.

He called out to them, 'Friends, haven't you any fish?'

'No,' they answered.

He said, 'Throw your net on the right side of the boat and you will find some.' When they did, they were unable to haul the net in because of the large number of fish.

Then the disciple whom Jesus loved said to Peter, 'It is the Lord!' As soon as Simon Peter heard him say, 'It is the Lord,' he wrapped his outer garment around him (for he had taken it off) and jumped into the water. The other disciples followed in the boat, towing the net full of fish, for they were not far from shore, about a hundred metres. When they landed, they saw a fire of burning coals there with fish on it, and some bread.

Jesus said to them, 'Bring some of the fish you have just caught.' So Simon Peter climbed back into the boat and dragged the net ashore. It was full of large fish, 153, but even with so many the net was not torn. Jesus said to them, 'Come and have breakfast.' None of the disciples dared ask him, 'Who are you?' They knew it was the Lord. Jesus came, took the bread and gave it to them, and did the same with the fish. This was now the third time Jesus appeared to his disciples after he was raised from the dead.

Remember to always make sure that fires are totally extinguished before you leave them or clear them away.

Sounds of silence

SERVICE

Focus: Stopping and listening for a while to the noise of the world around us to help us listen better to God.
Resources: None.

WE GATHER FOR WORSHIP

Welcome to our outdoor service. We are in this place today to be still for a while, to rest a moment in the arms of God and to hear what he may have to say to us.

So often we forget, and have conversations devoid of listening; and we fail to notice what is happening around us.

SONG

'Abba, Father, let me be', *Mission Praise*, 3
'God is here', *Hymns Ancient and Modern*, 464
'Come, satisfy us', *Songs of Fellowship*, 2250

WE SAY SORRY

Lord, for all the times when we allow the noise of the world to overtake us, we ask your forgiveness.

For all the times we fail to be still and hear your voice, we ask your forgiveness.

For all the times we choose not to listen but turn our heads away, we ask your forgiveness.

And for all the times when we put the concerns of the day above spending time with you, we ask your forgiveness.

WE ARE FORGIVEN

Lord, you are our comfort in times of need and yet so often we fail to listen to you.

Open our hearts, Lord, to hear your wisdom and let us hear you.

Give us peace in the day for your word to rest in our hearts, and help us to find the calm in the storm.

Lord, we listen to you now.
Amen.

WE AFFIRM OUR FAITH

We believe in one God,
the Father, the Almighty,
maker of heaven and earth,
of all that is, seen and unseen.

We believe in one Lord, Jesus Christ,
the only Son of God,
eternally begotten of the Father,
God from God, Light from Light,
true God from true God,
begotten, not made,
of one Being with the Father.
Through him all things were made.

For us and for our salvation
he came down from heaven:
by the power of the Holy Spirit
he became incarnate from the Virgin Mary,
and was made man.

For our sake he was crucified under Pontius Pilate;
he suffered death and was buried.

On the third day he rose again
in accordance with the Scriptures;
he ascended into heaven
and is seated at the right hand of the Father.

He will come again in glory to judge the living and the dead,
and his kingdom will have no end.

We believe in the Holy Spirit, the Lord, the giver of life,
who proceeds from the Father and the Son.
With the Father and the Son he is worshipped and glorified.
He has spoken through the Prophets.
We believe in one holy catholic and apostolic Church.
We acknowledge one baptism for the forgiveness of sins.
We look for the resurrection of the dead,
and the life of the world to come.
Amen.

SONG

'Be still and know that I am God', *Mission Praise*, 48
'This day God gives me', *Hymns Ancient and Modern*, 516
'On the day I called', *Songs of Fellowship*, 2488

READINGS

Psalm 46
   God is our refuge and strength,
      an ever-present help in trouble.
   Therefore we will not fear, though the earth give way
      and the mountains fall into the heart of the sea,
   though its waters roar and foam
      and the mountains quake with their surging.
   There is a river whose streams make glad the city of God,
      the holy place where the Most High dwells.
   God is within her, she will not fall;
      God will help her at break of day.
   Nations are in uproar, kingdoms fall;
      he lifts his voice, the earth melts.

The Lord Almighty is with us;
  the God of Jacob is our fortress.
Come and see what the Lord has done,
  the desolations he has brought on the earth.
He makes wars cease
  to the ends of the earth.
He breaks the bow and shatters the spear;
  he burns the shields with fire.
He says, 'Be still, and know that I am God;
  I will be exalted among the nations,
  I will be exalted in the earth.'
The Lord Almighty is with us;
  the God of Jacob is our fortress.

Matthew 11.28–30

'Come to me, all you who are weary and burdened, and I will give you rest. Take my yoke upon you and learn from me, for I am gentle and humble in heart, and you will find rest for your souls. For my yoke is easy and my burden is light.'

TALK

How often have you been having a conversation with someone only to realize that you have somehow tuned out and your mind has drifted to the latest football score or the shopping list?

Or worse – how often have you found yourself framing the next phrase in your discussion on an issue without listening to what the other person has been saying?

How often have you daydreamed without taking in what is going on around you?

Sometimes, in this world of noise, we have to make ourselves stop and listen.

We rarely hear silence any more; there is almost always some kind of noise.

Take a moment now to tune into what is happening around you and the noises that you can hear.

This is why this is a good activity to do out of doors as there will generally be a far wider range of noises. You may like to invite people to share what they have heard. Give this a good minute or two.

If we do not make time to listen then it is impossible for us to hear.

Listening takes discipline.

It takes courage, for in listening we open ourselves to that still, small voice of calm, the inner peace and wisdom that may well fly in the face of what we desire. We expose ourselves to the word and the will of God.

Silence is rare – a true absence of noise – so when we take a moment to be silent ourselves we must acknowledge the noise that happens around us. Acknowledge it and pass on, for we have a greater voice to listen for – the voice of God.

Be silent again and listen. Try to identify one sound, label it in your mind, then move on to the next; single it out, acknowledge it and move on. And when you have identified and named as many as you can, listen quietly for God.

Just being still and knowing that he is God is enough. Find your true rest in him. He does not speak in the words of men, or in the sounds of the world, but in the beating of our heart and the workings of our soul.

He may speak now but we may hear him later – but if we do not listen then we will never hear him.

Now remember this moment, this space to be near him. Look around and notice one thing – it might be a tree or a plant or a stone, a wall, a house or a car.

Use this as a visual reminder, and tell yourself that the next time you see this you will be reminded to listen – whether you are having a conversation with a friend, discussing a problem, rebuking a child or arguing a point.

If you do not listen then you cannot hear.

And if you do not make the time and the space to listen to God then you will not hear him.

WE SHARE THE PEACE

Lord, you create the perfect peace. Let us now share with one another a symbol of that peace.

SONG

'Be still for the presence of the Lord', *Mission Praise*, 50
'Be thou my vision', *Hymns Ancient and Modern*, 343
'And can it be that I should gain', *Songs of Fellowship*, 2215

WE PRAY TOGETHER

Lord, give us the grace to fall silent and hear your voice alone.
Lord, give us the grace to value others' words and thoughts above our own.
Lord, give us the grace to make space to listen and so to hear.
Lord, in your mercy,
Hear our prayer.

Lord, teach us your ways of compassion and wisdom.
Lord, teach us to be calm and at peace in you.
Lord, teach us to reach out to others with kindness.
Lord, in your mercy,
Hear our prayer.

Lord, keep us close to your side that we might look to you always.
Lord, keep us close to your side that we might follow only your pathway.
Lord, keep us close to your side that we may feel your abiding love.
Lord, in your mercy,
Hear our prayer.

Our Father in heaven
Hallowed be your name.
Your kingdom come
Your will be done
On earth as it is in heaven.
Give us today our daily bread
And forgive us our trespasses
As we forgive those who trespass against us.
Lead us not into temptation
But deliver us from evil.
For the kingdom, the power and the glory are yours
Now and for ever.
Amen.

WE GO INTO THE WORLD TOGETHER

So as we go out into the world, may we take the gift of silence with us to offer as our prayer.

May the grace of our Lord Jesus Christ guide and guard our tongues and may we respect the views of others, as we would wish others to respect our own.

David and Goliath

An activity where children create their own Goliath, then retell the Bible story through acting it out and firing water balloons (or foam balls) at their model of the giant.

Focus: The story of David and Goliath.
Type of activity: A Sunday school activity or as part of a family activity day.
Age range: 6 to 11 years.
Resources:
- A children's Bible.
- Materials to make the sections of the Goliath model – cardboard boxes, paper, paints, paint brushes.
- Ties to hold your boxes together such as string, plastic-covered wire (garden ties), bungie cords.
- Paper and pencils, and a catapult.
- A sling shot (water balloon launcher) or bungie cords and water balloons or foam balls to fire at the giant (with the optional extra of red powder paint).

Aim

For children to learn the story of David and Goliath and relate this to facing some big situations of their own.

Structure

Reading
Talking with the children
Making your giant
The outdoors bit
Bringing it together
Prayer

Reading

1 Samuel 17.1–50 (children's version)

Start your session by asking if anyone knows the story of David and Goliath – see what they can remember before you go through the full story. Then look at the story in a children's Bible picking out the following elements:

- Goliath was the champion of the Philistine army who were the enemies of King Saul and the Israelites.
- He was six cubits and a span tall – 2.9 metres.
- Every day Goliath shouted to the Israelites for someone to be sent to fight him. If someone could kill him the Philistines would become the subjects of the Israelites. He did this for 40 days.
- This made Saul and the Israelites scared.
- David's three eldest brothers fought in Saul's army but David was much younger and he tended his father's sheep.
- David was sent by his father to take some food – bread and cheese – to his brothers and to Saul.
- He arrived at the battle when it was the time that Goliath made one of his speeches.
- David persuaded Saul to let him face Goliath, even though he wasn't much more than a boy. After all, he had killed lions and bears in protecting his flock of sheep.
- David was dressed up by Saul in armour, but it was so heavy that he had to take it off.
- He then went and collected five stones from the river.
- Goliath didn't think much of being attacked by a boy but David was angry that Goliath had defied God. He took out his sling and a stone and fired a shot at Goliath.
- The stone hit Goliath in his forehead and he was killed.

With younger children you could read them the story from the children's Bible, showing them pictures of David and Goliath as you read it.

Talking with the children

Talk with the children about what it is like to be in a situation that seems really big, something that you are not sure you are going to be able to do or get over. Be careful how you address sensitive issues; use general examples rather than specifics if you are uncertain of where the conversation might go. You will be able to judge what is appropriate for your group, but topics could include: starting a new school, learning a new piece of music, reading in front of lots of people.

Discuss how David trusted in God and used his own skills to tackle Goliath in a way that others hadn't thought about – even though it looked like the soldiers had better equipment to defeat Goliath than he did.

The key message is that sometimes things can look really big and challenging and this can be a bit scary. So focus on what you can do and ask God for the strength to do the best you can to overcome the challenge in front of you, just like David did.

You are now going to make your own giant and retell the Bible story outside.

Making your giant

Goliath was 2.9 metres tall. The model can be made in sections, as follows. We know something about his battle dress and so we can estimate how large each of these elements might be:
- Goliath's head plus helmet – 60cm high. He wore a bronze helmet.
- His torso – 1.2m high. He wore a coat of scale armour of bronze.
- His arms – 1.1m long.
- His legs and feet – 1.3m long. He wore bronze greaves (pieces of armour to protect the shins).
- His weapons – he had a bronze javelin slung on his back and his spear shaft was a long rod with an iron point.

Don't worry about making your Goliath to the exact dimensions. It will depend on your resources, but it is quite nice to see how big he was.

Gather together the boxes and card you are going to use to make your giant. With the children decide which will be used for each part of his body. Cut out paper to fit each part of his body, for the children to draw or paint on.

Divide your children into groups. Share out the boxes, card and paper so that each group can produce one giant. They can use the descriptions from the Bible (above) as a reference. If you are working with younger children you may want to draw the outlines of the pictures for the children to colour in. Older children can make the pictures from scratch. It may depend on how much time you have available. (See colour photo of Goliath in the making on the website.)

When the pictures have been completed, stick the head and torso of your giant to the boxes. Stack these to form the top half of your giant. Stick your legs onto a large box, which goes at the bottom. For the arms cut out sheets of card to the right shape, then fix them onto the body using wire or plastic ties. Or you could use cardboard tubes. Then use ties to join all the body parts together to give them a bit of stability, although if you have a flat surface to build your giant on you may not need these. It will be easier to knock down your giant if the sections are not joined together. If it is windy you will need to secure the base of your giant. On grass you can use tent pegs to hold him down; on tarmac a couple of heavy weights in the bottom box may be enough to secure him. Or lean him up against a tree, wall or other structure, such as a stepladder.

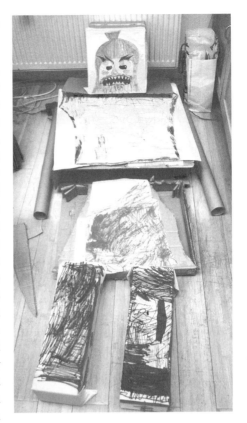

Goliath in the making

The outdoors bit

The main part of this activity is recreating key elements of the story of David and Goliath so that the children remember them. You want this to be an activity they will remember for a long time.

Choose one person to take the role of David, someone to be Saul, and three people to be David's brothers. You also need someone to voice Goliath's words as he challenges the Israelite army. Everyone else can be members of the Israelite army.

- If you have a large group, and plenty of time, you could make a section of the Philistine army using cardboard cutouts. Make individual soldier figures by having the children lie down on the card, and draw round them. These can be placed at the back of your space.

- Having created your Goliath, stand him up in front of your army.
- One of your group voices Goliath's words.
- You, as the Israelite army, cower in fear.
- David should be somewhere else tending his sheep, before coming to bring food to his brothers and Saul.
- Goliath makes another of his speeches.
- David goes to visit Saul and persuades him to let him fight Goliath.
- Saul gives David some armour, but David takes it off again before he leaves to face Goliath.
- David collects five stones from the river. You collect the water balloons or foam balls to fire at your Goliath figure using your sling.
- David goes to meet Goliath.
- David fires the sling (see below).

Firing your sling

Firing stones from a sling would be rather too dangerous, so get ready to fire the water balloons or foam balls. The best method is to use a three-man sling designed to fire water balloons. (See colour photo of firing a water balloon, on the website.) Bungie cords can also be used to fire them reasonably successfully. Test out beforehand how far you can fire your water balloons. It is likely to be between 10 and 30 metres so make sure you have enough space for the distance you are able to fire them.

Set up your giant in a place where any shots that miss are not going to hit anything or anyone they shouldn't. In front of a blank wall

Firing a water balloon

or hedge works well. Aim your water balloons or foam balls at your giant. If you use a little powder paint in your water or on your foam balls you will easily see where your shots have landed; use red and it will look like blood!

You will soon find out how skilful David must have been to hit Goliath in the head, just in the right place.

Remember to clear up the balloons and Goliath when you have finished.

Bringing it together

This is an activity that brings your story to life and one your children certainly won't forget.

At the end of the session, bring everyone together and go over the story. Ask them which bits they remember, and what they think it must have been like for David standing up to Goliath with just a small sling and a few stones. How important must it have been for him to be able to trust in God's strength?

Prayer

Ask the children to write down or draw a picture of something that is a challenge for them. They should then crumple up their paper into a ball without showing it to anyone else.

Use the catapult to fire your challenges as far away as you can. As each challenge is sent on its way ask the children to think about how God can help you feel strong when you face a tricky situation. Using God's strength can help you do more than you think you are able to do on your own – just like using the strength of other people to help you fire the sling!

Collect up your prayers, then either burn them or throw them away into your recycling (without looking at them).

Activities for any time of year

Sensing the quiet

Sitting quietly, children and young people note down the sounds they hear around them as a sound map, using their own symbols. This is a good activity to introduce them to quiet contemplation or prayer.

Focus: The beauty and variety of creation. As a starting point of learning, sitting in quiet contemplation or prayer.
Type of activity: It can be used at the beginning of a quiet day, during a time away together, or as part of a Sunday school activity.
Age range: 6 to 16 years.
Resources:
- Pieces of A5 card and pencils – one each.

Aim

To encourage quiet contemplation or prayer with a group who may not have done anything like this before.

Structure

About the activity
The outdoors bit
Following on

About the activity

Children often have noisy and sometimes chaotic lives. They have very few opportunities for taking time out and being quiet, especially without the distraction of technology. Being quiet can be quite a challenge. This activity, where they focus on something practical to do, can be a good introduction to taking time out of the hustle and bustle of the day to sit in quiet contemplation.

This activity aims to help children and young people engage with their environment more closely than they normally do – listening intently to explore the world around them. It can help them move on to thinking about being quiet in order to listen for God speaking to them in other ways through 'the still, small voice of calm'.

The outdoors bit

The children sit outside to 'collect' the different sounds. They should find themselves a comfortable space. On their piece of card they mark themselves in the middle of it.

They sit quietly and listen for a few minutes, marking on the card symbols to represent the sounds they hear, and indicating where the sounds are in relation to their position. Children should use their own symbols that remind them of the sounds: the louder the sound, the larger the symbol. So a car passing by could be a wavy line that gets bigger as it gets nearer and louder; the tweet of a bird could be represented by a tick or a v on the page. (See illustration on the website.)

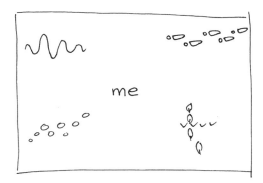

A sound map

After a set length of time, and when the children have finished making their sound maps, bring them together to discuss what they found. Start with simple, objective questions before asking the children to think about and share more personal thoughts. So you could ask first about the sounds they heard, and what symbols they used; which space was the quietest? Then you might move on to how sitting quietly made them feel. Have they ever done this before? Did it feel like a long time, or would they have been happy sitting there for longer? Were there any sounds they heard that they really liked that added to their experience?

Following on

Further questioning might help them to consider sitting quietly without the card in front of them. Could they still sit quietly? What else could they do while sitting quietly? They might think about something or someone special. They could pray. They could imagine the other people who have been in the space before them. Or think about what sounds they might like to add to their own quiet space.

End the activity by asking the children to sit quietly again in their outside space for a minute or two. This time they can choose what they do in that time – maybe something suggested in the discussions. They do not have to reveal what they are going to do – this is their own quiet time and they should feel comfortable in their space.

You could repeat this activity on other occasions if it works well. As the children get used to sitting in silence you can extend the time to five minutes then maybe to ten minutes, depending on their age and how they progress through this activity.

Progressing this further, you can lead a walk around a space, dropping off people on the journey. Make sure everyone is carrying something to sit on (a carpet tile, or a newspaper inside a plastic bag). Lead the group on a journey around your space and every few metres one person sits down, and the rest of the group move on. Carry on until everyone is sitting quietly, near enough to see the next person but far enough away to feel alone in their space. After a few minutes go back to the beginning of your journey and walk along the route picking everyone up as you go. This can be a way of discovering a new site, maybe on a church day or weekend away. Or it could be finishing something off by giving everyone space to be quiet and reflect on the activities that they have taken part in together.

Post boxes

A relay race game that can be used to review and remind children and young people about something they have been learning about.

Focus: Reviewing work done in Sunday school or youth group, or during a time away together.

Type of activity: A fun game to remind everyone of what they have been looking at over a session or a number of weeks.

Age range: 6 to 16 years.

Resources:

- Five or more boxes with slots for posting cards through. Each box is marked with a category or 'answer' relating to the subject of the activity (see below).
- A selection of cards or 'letters' showing clues and information relating to the categories on the boxes.
- A pencil.

Aim

To remind children and young people of what they have been studying in a fun way.

Structure

Choosing the topic
Setting things up
The outdoors bit

Choosing the topic

Choose any topic that you have been working on that will give you a range of categories or 'answer' words on the subject. Mark one of these words on each box so that they are clear to see. Then make cards or 'letters', with a clue word or phrase written on them that matches one of the boxes (or more than one). So if

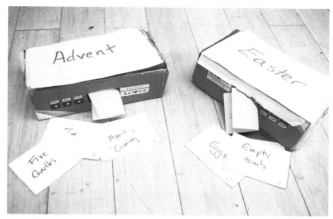

Post boxes

you had 'Easter' written on a box, your 'letters' might read, for example, 'He is risen', 'Empty tomb' or 'Eggs'. (See colour photo of post boxes on the website.) Prepare at least five boxes, each with a different answer category, and lots of cards with information to match each box. See the specific example below, which is about Christian festivals. Other topics might be:

- The ten commandments.
- New Testament books.
- Old Testament characters.
- Parables.
- The sayings of Jesus.
- The disciples.

Setting things up

For a review of Christian festivals, the five boxes – these need not be big, just large enough to 'post' your letters into – should each be marked with the name of a Christian festival: Advent, Christmas, Lent, Easter, Harvest. These need to be clearly visible.

Create the 'letters', showing as many things as you can think of related to each of the festivals. You need enough so that everyone has to deliver at least two letters – probably more. Use one item per letter, but you can also repeat answers several times. Tailor the questions to the age of your participants. You could use pictures instead if literacy levels are an issue.

- **Advent** – five candles, means 'coming', calendar, doors, beginning of church year.
- **Christmas** – stable, star, manger, twelve days, 25 December.
- **Lent** – Ash Wednesday, giving things up, forty days, Jesus in the wilderness.
- **Easter** – empty tomb, resurrection, the end of Holy Week, movable feast, eggs.
- **Harvest** – crops, we plough the fields and scatter, thanksgiving for crops, gifts of food.

Place the boxes well spread out around the outside space. They need to be far enough apart so that people have to move to get from one to another. They should be visible but you should not be able to see what is on them from a distance.

Divide the participants into teams, and each team is given a number. This means that their letters and their deliveries can be tracked. You will need a central person in charge of handing out the letters to the teams. This person has all the letters to be delivered at the 'depot'.

The outdoors bit

This is a relay race. The first member of each team comes to the central depot to collect a letter. Their team number is written on the letter. At the beginning, send someone from every team out together; then after that it will depend on how quickly they deliver their letters. The task for each person is to deliver their card to the appropriate box, then return to their team. The next member of their team collects a letter, their team number is put on the back of the letter, and off they go to deliver it.

You can have a number of letters with the same clue on, or a selection of clues that could belong in more than one box, to make the game a little trickier. You could have enough cards for everyone to deliver half a dozen letters each, depending on their energy and speed.

When the cards have run out (or your participants have run out of energy) collect up the boxes. Count the number of correct answers in each one, and the team with the most answers in the correct boxes is the winner.

Baking and breaking bread outside

Baking bread over an open fire then sharing it together. This is especially good for a youth group or confirmation class learning about the sacraments.

Focus: Thinking about the significance of breaking and sharing bread together as a community by making bread to share together.
Type of activity: An activity for a youth group or confirmation group session or as part of time away together.
Age range: A confirmation group or youth group.
Resources:

- A barbecue or camp fire, a flat baking tray or shallow frying pan that can be used over a fire, barbecue tongs or similar.
- A recipe for making bread that can be baked on a fire – a selection are given below.
- Bread ingredients, mixing bowl, utensils and a work surface.
- Picnic blankets or low seats to sit on around the fire.
- A bucket of water and a first aid kit.
- A roll of lining paper.

Aim

To develop a greater understanding of the importance of sharing communion.

Structure

Introduction
Cooking on an open fire
Recipes
Facilitating a discussion
Sharing the bread
Drawing with charcoal from the fire

Introduction

Gather everyone together, around the fire if you have lit one, and provide an overview of what you are going to be doing throughout the session. Go over health and safety issues, as outlined in the health and safety section of this book.

Start by reading the story of the Last Supper.

Mark 14.12–26

On the first day of the Festival of Unleavened Bread, when it was customary to sacrifice the Passover lamb, Jesus' disciples asked him, 'Where do you want us to go and make preparations for you to eat the Passover?'

So he sent two of his disciples, telling them, 'Go into the city, and a man carrying a jar of water will meet you. Follow him. Say to the owner of the house he enters, "The Teacher asks: Where is my guest room, where I may eat the Passover with my disciples?" He will show you a large room upstairs, furnished and ready. Make preparations for us there.'

The disciples left, went into the city and found things just as Jesus had told them. So they prepared the Passover.

When evening came, Jesus arrived with the Twelve. While they were reclining at the table eating, he said, 'Truly I tell you, one of you will betray me – one who is eating with me.'

They were saddened, and one by one they said to him, 'Surely you don't mean me?'

'It is one of the Twelve,' he replied, 'one who dips bread into the bowl with me. The Son of Man will go just as it is written about him. But woe to that man who betrays the Son of Man! It would be better for him if he had not been born.'

While they were eating, Jesus took bread, and when he had given thanks, he broke it and gave it to his disciples, saying, 'Take it; this is my body.'

Then he took a cup, and when he had given thanks, he gave it to them, and they all drank from it.

'This is my blood of the covenant, which is poured out for many,' he said to them. 'Truly I tell you, I will not drink again from the fruit of the vine until that day when I drink it new in the kingdom of God.'

When they had sung a hymn, they went out to the Mount of Olives.

This age group will be starting to take communion and may be learning about this in confirmation classes. They are likely to be familiar with the story of the Last Supper and why they receive bread in communion. However, by taking time to make the bread themselves and creating something that is shared, they can learn how this sacrament is important within the church family.

Different churches may see the breaking and sharing of bread in different ways. We are assuming that the bread baked here will be shared among the young people, but it could also be consecrated and used in a service with the wider church community.

Cooking on an open fire

See the health and safety information within this book and the information about working with fire.

You can use a barbecue or similar container to hold your fire, or create a pit in the ground, by cutting away a section of turf. Use something that you can clear away afterwards, so that others are not encouraged to light fires in your grounds. (See colour photo of gathering around a fire wok on the website.)

Gathering around a fire wok

It is fun to start a fire without matches or paper – this is much easier than it may sound. Cotton wool is a great tinder material; place a few balls of it, teased out slightly, at the base of your pit or container. Then use a fire steel to create a spark which will (probably with a few attempts) set the cotton wool alight. To operate a fire steel (available from camping shops or online) use the thumb holes and hold the small sheet of metal at about 45 degrees to the rod, then push it away from you and towards the cotton wool. Push hard against the rod, holding its base near to the cotton wool and you should see sparks which will light the tinder. (See colour photo of using a fire steel on the website.)

Using a fire steel

To get your fire going you will need a range of sizes of pieces of dry wood. Start your fire with a bundle of fine twigs, lit from your cotton wool, and gradually build your fire by adding larger and larger twigs and logs, without smothering the flames.

To cook your bread you will need to let the fire die down to glowing embers, as direct flames will burn your bread on the outside and not cook it in the middle. So make sure you light your fire early, so that it has a chance to die down before you are wanting to use it.

When you are ready to bake your bread, preheat the tray or pan then place the dough on it over the fire. Cooking times will vary. Turn the loaves occasionally and tear off a piece to check that they are cooked inside.

Recipes

Three recipes for bread to cook over a fire are included here. Choose the one that fits your group and the time you have available, or research others.

Bannock bread

The dough is often wound around sticks to be cooked over an open fire, but it can also be made into shapes more like flat bread, and cooked on a baking tray or in a frying pan over a fire (or make your own structure, as in the photo). Using cups is a good way of measuring ingredients when you are outside.

Bannock bread

3 cups flour
1 tsp baking powder
1 tsp salt
½ cup dry milk powder
1 cup water

Mix the ingredients together in a bowl to make your dough. Create a number of flattened loaves or rolls and cook these over your fire on your baking tray or in your pan. (See colour photo of bannock bread on the website.)

Soda bread

500g flour
½ tsp salt
1½ tsp of bicarbonate of soda
400ml buttermilk or plain yoghurt

Mix the ingredients together (do not knead them) and shape them into relatively flat loaves or rolls. Sprinkle some flour over your tray or pan. Place your dough on the tray over the fire and turn the loaves occasionally until a firm crust forms.

Jewish flat bread

5½ cups plain flour
1 tbsp salt
1 tbsp sugar
1 packet active dry yeast
2 cups warm water
Oil to grease your bowl and a damp cloth

Put the flour into a bowl and add salt. Mix your sugar and yeast with the warm water then pour these into your dry ingredients. Mix these together then knead them for about 5 minutes. Let the dough rest, then knead it again for another 5 minutes. Grease your bowl and put your dough back inside. Cover with a damp cloth and leave until it has risen to twice its size. This can take up to two hours.

Remove your dough and knead it again for 2 to 3 minutes, then divide it into several pieces and shape them into balls. Let these rise for about 20 minutes, then place your baking tray or pan over the fire to heat up. Sprinkle this with flour or cornmeal, then place a ball of dough in the centre. With wet hands, spread the dough to flatten it out (be careful not to touch the hot pan – alternatively you can stretch the dough before placing it on the tray). Bake for about 15 minutes.

Facilitating a discussion

Gathering around the fire is a natural way to bring everyone together in an informal way. The aim of this activity is to explore why the bread in communion might be important for them and other people within their church community.

Start by recalling the story of the Last Supper. You can do this in a number of ways:

- Read the Bible story directly.
- Take it in turns to tell the story; each person says one line in turn as you go around the circle.
- Working in small groups, the young people tell the story in any way they want – they could perform it as a mini-play, or as a mime, write a poem, or a song, create a comic strip, etc.
- Ask questions of the group to tease out the story from them.

Ask them to identify the elements of the story that are important to them, or ones they can identify with. They might pick out any of the following:

- It was a group of friends coming together to share a meal.
- One person there was saying goodbye to the rest of them (even if they didn't know it at the time).
- One of the group was going to betray their leader.
- Their leader shared bread and wine with the group.
- The bread and wine represented Jesus' body and blood.
- The bread and wine represented the forgiveness of sins.
- The group sang hymns together.

Sharing the bread

Creating kennings

Kennings are two-word phrases that describe something without saying what it is. A kenning about a fire might be 'glowing brightly' or 'ember making'.

Ask the group to come up with kennings about the bread they have made and are about to share. Some ideas might be 'life giving' or 'sustaining food'. They could share their kennings with the whole group.

When you are sharing the bread you have made, instead of the usual 'the body of Christ' the group can use the kennings they have created as they tear off and present a piece of bread to the person sitting next to them.

Songs

As the disciples did at the end of the Last Supper, your group can join together in singing hymns or songs:

'I am the bread of life', *Mission Praise*, 260
'Broken for you', *Mission Praise*, 66
'Jesus, stand among us', *Mission Praise*, 381

Drawing with charcoal from the fire

As a conclusion to the activity the group can use the charcoal created by the fire, once it has cooled, to draw an image of what they have done and discussed, for example on wallpaper lining paper. Or you could gather the charcoal and use it later to remind everyone of the activity and their time together. You can create charcoal by dousing the embers with water before they have completely turned to ashes.

The group can either create one large image of the whole story, or divide into smaller groups to work on different elements. Or, create images that reflect other aspects of the session, such as the kennings.

As always when using fire – make sure it is completely extinguished, or cleared away, before you leave.

A Bible story in a box

Creating pictures in boxes telling a Bible story using materials collected from the outdoor environment.

Focus: A parable or other Bible story.
Type of activity: Sunday school activity or part of an activity day for children or young people.
Age range: 6 to 16 years.
Resources:
- A selection of boxes of a mixture of sizes.
- Access to natural materials.
- Alternatively, use man-made items such as coloured paper, glue, paint, and other art materials – or a mixture of natural and man-made materials. It will depend on the story you choose and the location of your scenes.

Aim

To create a trail of scenes that depict a Bible story that can be displayed outside.

Structure

Choosing your story
Selecting the scenes
The outdoors bit
    Selecting the locations to display the boxes
    Creating the scenes
    Displaying your story

Choosing your story

Choose any Bible story that can be divided into a number of scenes. The example described here is the story of Noah (Genesis 6.9–9.17). The key parts of the story are listed below. You could use a children's version of the Bible depending on the age group you are working with.

Your story needs to have a clear and simple structure, with several sections or locations so that you can make a picture for each scene.

Selecting the scenes

The number of scenes you choose to depict will depend on the structure of the story, and the size of your group who are making the scenes. For the story of Noah, 12 scenes works well, as below. You could alternatively select just a few key elements from the story.

- 6.11–12: The people on the earth were being bad.
- 6.14–16: God told Noah to make an ark of cypress wood, 135 metres long and 22.5 metres wide, with a door in the side and upper and lower decks.
- 6.19–20: God told Noah to bring two of every animal to the ark – one male and one female.
- 7.10: Seven days later it began to rain.
- 7.17–19: It rained for 40 days and 40 nights. Gradually the water rose up the sides of the mountains and covered the earth.
- 8.3–5: After 150 days the waters started to recede, until the tops of the mountains became visible.
- 8.6–7: After another 40 days Noah sent out a raven.
- 8.8–9: Then Noah sent out a dove to search for dry ground – but it found nowhere to perch.
- 8.10–11: After another seven days he sent out the dove again, and it returned with an olive leaf.
- 8.12: After another seven days he sent it out again and this time it did not return.
- 8.13–14: The earth gradually dried out and Noah and his family came out of the ark, as did all the animals.
- 9.12–13: After the flood God promised never to destroy all the living things again and he set a rainbow in the sky as a sign of his promise.

The outdoors bit

Selecting the locations to display the boxes

In this case your 12 scenes will be displayed in 12 different locations. Allocate scenes to individuals or pairs of children or young people, ask them to choose a box, then take everything outside.

With the group, work out a route for your display of boxes so that the story can be told as you follow the trail. Create a plan or map of the route so that it is easy for others to follow. This also means you can be flexible about where the boxes are located around the site, rather than just following an existing pathway.

Creating the scenes

Each person, pair or group with a box then creates their scene in the box. Using boxes gives a frame to work within; people often find making smaller creations easier than large ones. And, of course, the boxes give shelter for outside display.

A diverse natural environment may offer enough materials for everyone to use what they can find around them to create their scene, but it may be useful to add man-made art materials to the mix. You could populate your scenes with model figures, as well as other objects, if this will help you tell the story. (See colour photos of dry land and rainbow of colours in a box on the website.)

Dry land in a box

Rainbow of colours in a box

Displaying your story

Display your finished boxes along the route. Walking the route, the scenes take you through the story. You can let people discover the story just through the images in the boxes as they walk around the trail. Or to supplement the scenes, you could do one of the following.

- Write out Bible verses, laminate them and display them next to each of the boxes.
- Use your map of the route to link the boxes and relevant verses to their locations on the map.

As this is a temporary display, take photographs of the boxes and display the story inside for a longer period of time.

Creating and walking a labyrinth

Making a temporary labyrinth and undertaking a contemplative walk, recreating an activity that has been carried out in churches for centuries.

Focus: A time for quiet contemplation.
Type of activity: An activity that all can take part in over a few days or perhaps weeks.
Age range: All ages.
Resources:
- Instructions for how to make a labyrinth (see illustration on page 147), and materials to make it with (see below for suggestions).
- Cards with Bible passages or other thoughts written on, or images.

Structure

About labyrinths
The outdoors bit – creating the labyrinth

About labyrinths

Labyrinths have been created by many cultures for centuries and can be found all over the world. A labyrinth differs from a maze in that it follows just one pathway, with no junctions and choices; it is not usually a puzzle to be solved, whereas a maze is. The earliest example of a labyrinth in a church is at El Asnam in Algeria, which dates back to the fourth century, and follows the traditional Roman labyrinth pattern.

Some churches in Italy and France contain pavement labyrinth designs; there are also examples in Belgium and Germany. The most famous is probably the thirteenth-century labyrinth at Chartres Cathedral in France. Labyrinths were used as a way of doing penance, or as a substitute for pilgrimages to distant places, especially for the infirm or those otherwise unable to travel. They were also used for other rituals that included choral dancing.

Today Christians often use labyrinths as a metaphor for human life, as a contemplative pathway to follow while meditating. This is how we use the labyrinth in this activity. You could choose some appropriate music to accompany the walk, and to help set the contemplative mood if you undertake this activity at home.

The outdoors bit – creating the labyrinth

Instructions for creating a three-ring labyrinth are given in the illustration. Start by setting out four markers then create the pathways in the order illustrated.

Making a three-ring labyrinth

Suggestions for materials that can be used to mark out the pathway outside include:

- Strips of cloth about 10cm wide (old sheets or duvet covers are perfect for this).
- Pebbles.
- Chalk lines on a hard surface. You could also draw mini labyrinths on walls or on paving stones which you can follow with a finger.

- Lay black plastic on grass and secure it in place. You can leave it down for about three weeks without permanently damaging the grass. When you remove it the grass will be yellow where the plastic has been, but will gradually turn back to green over time.
- Light candles or lanterns to mark out your path. Obviously you need to be careful with safety but this can be very effective in the dusk and dark.
- Mow the path in grass, allowing the grass to grow up along the pathway edges.
- For a permanent labyrinth, cut the design into turf, possibly adding gravel to create the path. It will be easy to maintain if the labyrinth is walked regularly.

Walking a labyrinth

In order to help people walking the labyrinth to focus their thoughts, place poems, prayers, Bible verses or images along the walk. One idea would be to take the theme of the natural world. Make sure these are spread along the route so that your path doesn't appear too crowded. Also consider how people will leave the labyrinth once they reach the centre. If you have enough space you can ask everyone to retrace their steps along the path to return to the entrance. (See colour photo of walking a labyrinth on the website.)

Examples of Bible verses focusing on the natural world include:

- **Psalm 24.1:** The earth is the Lord's, and everything in it, the world, and all who live in it.
- **Colossians 1.16:** For in him all things were created: things in heaven and on earth, visible and invisible, whether thrones or powers or rulers or authorities; all things have been created through him and for him.
- **Psalm 89.11:** The heavens are yours, and yours also the earth; you founded the world and all that is in it.
- **John 1.3:** Through him all things were made; without him nothing was made that has been made.
- **Psalm 104.25:** There is the sea, vast and spacious, teeming with creatures beyond number – living things both large and small.

- **Psalm 19.1:** The heavens declare the glory of God; the skies proclaim the work of his hands.

At the centre of your labyrinth, where the path is leading to, you could place an added feature. On Good Friday, for example, you could have a cross at the centre. Pebbles could be placed at each stopping point, which could be picked up and carried to the centre of the labyrinth, then placed to form a cairn. These can represent your thoughts and prayers being laid at the foot of the cross.

You can also accompany your walking of the labyrinth with some contemplative music.

Creating a church timeline

Making an outdoor timeline of your church's year, by attaching dates of feasts, festivals and the other events your church runs along a length of washing line or rope and hanging onto it the different events.

Focus: Understanding the pattern of the church year.
Type of activity: For use with a children's group, youth group or confirmation class. Adults being introduced to the church might find it useful too.
Age range: Children aged 6 to 16, or adults new to the church.
Resources:
- A length of washing line, rope or cloth strip (see the section on putting together your outdoor church kit).
- Pieces of thin card showing your church festivals. You could make these as part of the activity. These could also be laminated.
- Clothes pegs, or hole punch and string.

Aim

For people to learn, or be reminded of, the pattern of the church year.

Structure

Getting ready
The outdoors bit

Getting ready

You need to create cards showing the different feasts, holy days and other events in your church year. As well as words it might be good to use symbols or pictures representing each event. Choose A4 or A5 cards, depending on the space available.

First decide on the number of events you are going to hang on your timeline. Include things that are specific to your church, if possible, such as your church fete, Christmas fair or patronal festival, along with general church festivals such as Lent and Easter. The following is a list of dates you could include with their place in the year of the Western Church.

- The four Sundays before Christmas – Advent.
- 25 December – Christmas Day.
- 6 January – Epiphany.
- 46 days before Easter – Ash Wednesday, the start of Lent.
- Sunday before Easter – Palm Sunday.
- The week leading up to Easter – Holy Week.
- The Thursday before Easter – Maundy Thursday.
- The Friday before Easter – Good Friday.
- March/April – Easter Day.
- The fortieth day after Easter – Ascension Day.
- Fifty days after Easter Sunday – Pentecost (Whit Sunday).
- First Sunday after Pentecost – Trinity Sunday.
- 1 November – All Saints Day.

You could prepare the cards before you do the activity, or make them either at one session, or over the year as you celebrate each event, or during a course introducing Christianity. Using them all together at the end of your year, or course, could represent a revision activity.

For each festival or feast, include the event name or draw and perhaps paste on a picture or symbol to represent it. If you are able, laminate your cards so they will last a lot longer outside.

The outdoors bit

Make sure your washing line or rope is long enough to include all your cards. Decide where the best place is to hang it. How long is it going to stay up, and who else is going to use the space? Can you put it where visitors to your church can see it, or so that it can be viewed as people pass by?

Decide where in the year you are to begin your timeline. Traditionally the church year starts with Advent, so that is the best card to have at the beginning.

Attach the cards using clothes pegs, or punch holes in the cards, thread string through and tie them onto the line.

If working with younger groups you could peg up key festivals like Christmas and Easter in advance and ask them to fill in the gaps.

Here are some other ways you can carry out this activity.

- Hand out the ready-made cards and ask the group to put them into the right order.
- Have two (or more) clothes lines and complete sets of cards, and run it as a relay race.
- Set the cards up on the line but in any old order and ask the group(s) to arrange them correctly.
- You could do this activity by laying cards out on the ground, if hanging them up is not an option.

Graveyard exploration

Using your graveyard to learn more about the history of your community by undertaking an exploration quiz or a scavenger hunt.

Focus: To learn about the church community over the years and to have fun!
Type of activity: An activity for Sunday school or a uniformed organization. An older group such as a youth club could plan the clues for a younger group.
Age range: Primary-aged children; with more difficult clues the activity would also be suitable for older children or even adults.
Resources:
- A graveyard.
- Copies of the questions, pencils and clipboards.

Aim

To make connections with your history of your church community and to find out more about your churchyard.

Structure

Planning
The outdoors bit
A scavenger hunt

Planning

This could be extended to your whole church grounds but the description here is just for your graveyard.

The research and planning for this activity could be undertaken by one group for another group, for example the youth group could create the quiz or make it into a treasure hunt for younger children. If you have someone who is particularly good at creating quiz clues, ask them to help you plan yours.

For each church the activity will be different – these are a few ideas to get you going.

- Can you find a gravestone commemorating someone who lived to over 90? Who were they and when did they live?
- Can you find a gravestone with at least two different types of lichen on it? Whose gravestone is it? (See colour photo of gravestones on the website.)
- Can you find four gravestones with the same surname on? What were their first names?
- How many trees are there in your graveyard?
- What species of tree is at the entrance to the graveyard?
- What does the tallest gravestone look like?
- How many angels do you have on gravestones in your graveyard?
- Can you find a gravestone of a husband and wife?

Lichen on gravestones

- Can you find someone who worked with their hands? Who were they and what did they do?
- What is the longest name you can find?
- Can you find anyone who was a parent and a grandparent? What was their name?
- Can you find someone with the same name as you or someone else you know in the church community? When did they live?

To ensure that everyone enjoys themselves make sure that the majority of the questions are straightforward to answer; but do include some trickier ones too or else you won't be able to find a winner!

You need to have enough clipboards, copies of the questions and pencils for those taking part, either for people to work in groups or individually.

The outdoors bit

Hand out the questions. Remind everyone of the hazards in the graveyard, such as uneven ground, overhead branches, fallen gravestones, before you send them off on the hunt.

You could set a time limit, saying that points will be taken off for those coming in outside the time, or bonus ones added to those who finish ahead of everyone else.

A scavenger hunt

Alternatively you could turn this into a scavenger hunt, asking people to collect certain items found in your church grounds. You will need bags or boxes for them to collect their items in, and other resources such as paper and wax crayons for rubbings. A few ideas of items to collect are:

- Leaves from five different types of tree or bush.
- Rubbings from two gravestones.
- A round stone.
- Something blue.
- The longest blade of grass you can find.
- Something man-made.

You could vary the number of points awarded for different items, with easier ones being worth less than those more difficult to find. This will help you sort out your winners.

Sensing a story

Telling a story and adding sensory experiences to its telling, to deepen the experience. This is a particularly good activity for those with disabilities or special needs. For this example we use the parable of the sower.

Focus: To retell a Bible story in a way that helps participants to experience it using different senses.

Type of activity: An activity in which people work in pairs. During the telling of the Bible story, one person creates a range of sensory experiences, enhancing the telling of the story, for the other person.

Age range: Suitable for all ages, from the very young to the very old.

Resources:
- A copy of the story you are going to tell in a form suitable for your group.
- Identical sets of sensory materials for each pair of participants. You can collect these as part of the activity or prepare them beforehand. An example set of resources, for the parable of the sower, is outlined below.

Aim

For participants in pairs to each experience a Bible story more deeply by using their senses in different ways.

Structure

How the activity works
Planning
The outdoors bit
    Making the collection part of the activity
    Telling the story

How the activity works

A leader, or other member of the group, reads out the story. Everyone else sits in pairs, with one person experiencing the story while the other creates the sensory effects. The receiver has their eyes shut and their hands out in front of them, palms upwards. The giver has to create sensory experiences that reflect the story as it is read and make it more real.

The storyteller has an assistant who models the actions, which everyone copies, so that all the receivers get the same experience.

If you were telling the story of Jesus calming the storm, for example, the receiver might experience the wind and rain through being fanned by a large leaf and being splattered with drops of water!

Planning

The first thing you need to do is choose your story. Here we have chosen the parable of the sower.

Matthew 13.3–23

Then he told them many things in parables, saying: 'A farmer went out to sow his seed. As he was scattering the seed, some fell along the path, and the birds came and ate it up. Some fell on rocky places, where it did not have much soil. It sprang up quickly, because the soil was shallow. But when the sun came up, the plants were scorched, and they withered because they had no root. Other seed fell among thorns, which grew up and choked the plants. Still other seed fell on good soil, where it produced a crop – a hundred, sixty or thirty times what was sown. Whoever has ears, let them hear.'

The disciples came to him and asked, 'Why do you speak to the people in parables?'

He replied, 'Because the knowledge of the secrets of the kingdom of heaven has been given to you, but not to them. Whoever has will be given more, and they will have an abundance. Whoever does not have, even what they have will be taken from them. This is why I speak to them in parables:

"Though seeing, they do not see;
though hearing, they do not hear or understand."

In them is fulfilled the prophecy of Isaiah:

"You will be ever hearing but never understanding;
you will be ever seeing but never perceiving.
For this people's heart has become calloused;
they hardly hear with their ears,
and they have closed their eyes.
Otherwise they might see with their eyes,
hear with their ears,
understand with their hearts
and turn, and I would heal them."

'But blessed are your eyes because they see, and your ears because they hear. For truly I tell you, many prophets and righteous people longed to see what you see but did not see it, and to hear what you hear but did not hear it.

'Listen then to what the parable of the sower means: when anyone hears the message about the kingdom and does not understand it, the evil one comes and snatches away what was sown in their heart. This is the seed sown along the path. The seed falling on rocky ground refers to someone who hears the word and at once receives it with joy. But since they have no root, they last only a short time. When trouble or persecution comes because of the word, they quickly fall away. The seed falling among the thorns refers to someone who hears the word, but the worries of this life and the deceitfulness of wealth choke the word, making it unfruitful. But the seed falling on good soil refers to someone who hears the word and understands it. This is the one who produces a crop, yielding a hundred, sixty or thirty times what was sown.'

This is the NIV version of the story. Depending on the age or ability of your group, you might want to use a different version such as from a children's Bible.

The items you collect need to make the story come alive. Many could be found in your grounds. You can make the collection of the items part of the activity, or have everything prepared beforehand.

To tell the parable of the sower you might include:

• The sower scattering the seed – you will need some seeds, ideally collected from outdoors, but you could use any.
• They fall upon the path and the birds eat them up – use two little twigs each to form the beaks of the birds, or you could use clothes pegs.
• Some fell on rocky soil – collect some pebbles.
• Some fell among thorns – something a little spiky such as thorny twigs or holly leaves.

- Some fell on good soil – a small sample of soil.
- For the crop, whether growing or withering – long stems of grass or wheat.
- You might also like to add some water to represent rain.

Remember that you need one set of items for each pair of people who are taking part.

The outdoors bit

Making the collection part of the activity

You can involve people in a number of different ways:

- All work together to decide on the different materials you need to collect, then each pair collects one set of prescribed items, or each pair collects all of one of the items, enough for everyone to use.
- Each pair decides on their own items to collect and gets everything they need. In this case everyone's experience of the story will be slightly different.
- Each pair is assigned one sensory experience, and they decide what they will collect, then go out and find enough sets for everyone.

Telling the story

Put all the items that you have collected to help tell the story onto a plate or tray for each pair so that they are easy to pick up and use as you tell the story. (See colour photo of items for the story on the website.)

Items for the story

Pairs position themselves so that one partner can provide the experiences to the other – sitting opposite each other, or one could be sitting and the other standing.

The storyteller should be located where everyone can easily hear them speak. You could spread out in a quiet area outside, with the storyteller seated in the middle of the group.

The person providing the experiences has their items beside them ready to use and needs to be facing the storyteller and their assistant. Their partner should have their eyes closed for the whole activity, and holds their hands out in front, palms upwards.

While the leader reads out the story their assistant shows those providing the sensory experiences what they need to do and when – making the story more real to the person experiencing it.

For the parable of the sower, the activity would go like this.

- A sower goes out to sow – the giver gently scatters a few seeds into the receiver's hands.
- It lands on the path and the birds come and eat it up – use two sticks (or clothes peg) to make little pinches on their hands, as if pecking up the seed.
- More seeds are sown – scatter more seeds.
- These land on stony ground – place a few pebbles into their hands. They can rub the pebbles to feel them better.
- These start to grow well but there is not enough soil so they soon wither and die – wipe the long stems of grass across their palms, then pull them away as they wither.
- More seeds are sown – scatter more seeds.
- These seeds land among thorns that choke them and stop them from growing – carefully scratch thorns across their palms.
- Finally sow some more seeds – scatter more seeds.
- These land in good soil – add some soil to their hands.
- It rains and the sun shines – sprinkle with water.
- The crop grows well – give the grass stems to your partner to hold.
- It produces seed one hundred, sixty or thirty times what was sown – pour in the remainder of your seeds.

Repeat the storytelling with the partners switching roles, so each person experiences the sensory story.

Your next steps

Making your outside spaces the best they can be

If you want to increase your options about getting outside you may want to think about developing your grounds to enable this to happen more often and more easily. This section leads you through the process of planning changes to your site, whether on a temporary basis or permanently.

Focus: Changing spaces for a purpose, whether temporary or long term, for small or large groups. How you can get people involved, what you need to consider and how you can make it happen.

Who is it for? Your whole church community. A group leading the process will be useful to keep things on track, especially if it is a large project that incorporates permanent change.

Activity resources:

- For the consultation and planning – large sheets of paper, pens, pencils, scissors, sticky notes, glue, etc. Ask those involved to collect images of spaces they both like and don't like – perhaps out of magazines, or photographs of places they have visited.
- For planning on the ground – useful items could include ropes or long strips of cloth, carpet tiles, flowerpots, pieces of wood or stones, bamboo canes, chairs.
- For temporary changes – you could use any of the following: sheets, tarpaulins and blankets, flowers, stones and pebbles, pictures or sculptures, bales of straw, outdoor bean bags or cushions, chairs, tables.
- For permanent change – you will find this out once you have undergone your consultation and design process.

Why change an outside space?

An outside space is often on view to the public, so your space should be part of your witness as a church, although it is somewhere that might not be seen as 'church'. Some people may be wary of entering a church building, but find it easier to join you in an outdoor space. It will generally be more informal, with none of the 'strange' features that churches often have inside. It is easy to come and go from an outside space, which means that people won't feel trapped. Overall, outside spaces can be less threatening and more welcoming for many people.

Whether you are creating a special space just for one service or activity, or are thinking of somewhere more permanent, the principles for working out what you might do are much the same. However, in this section we have separated out quick, temporary changes from those that might apply to a larger space and last longer. You are not likely to spend as much time planning if the space is going to change for just a short length of time as you would for a permanent change.

It is worth taking as much time as you can, especially if you are planning long-term change, or you are committing money to the development of the space. However much time you have available, making the most of this will help you create a space that works for you.

Whether you have yet to decide on a specific space, or how to develop it, or whether you already have a space in mind and know exactly what you want to achieve, take a deep breath, gather a working group together and move forward one step at a time. That extra bit of time spent planning is always well worth the effort, rather than rushing into making changes too quickly.

How to get people involved

Small, temporary changes to a space will probably only involve the people who are going to use the space on that one occasion. But significant changes are likely to affect a wider range of people, so it is important that they are given an opportunity to have some input. A working group will be useful to coordinate things and keep progress on track.

You might want to start by giving a presentation to your whole church community about what you are thinking of doing (for example, that you want to use a particular space for a purpose that is likely to involve change, without being specific about the changes at this stage) and this would be a good time to recruit your working group.

The working group should be a good representation of your church community, young and old, to broaden perspective and bring diverse skills and knowledge to bring to the project.

At each stage in your project there will be other ways to get people involved. This might just be an opinion, or it might be active involvement. Asking individuals directly for ideas and help will always be more profitable than a general appeal for help, while making events or occasions fun will also encourage people to get on board.

Look at what you've got

Begin by taking a good look at the different spaces you have access to, whether these are around your church or further afield. Are they suitable, and are they easy for everyone to get to? Do they lend themselves to a particular use or could they be adapted for lots of activities? You may not need to change physical features at all, just the way the space is used; don't make changes just for the sake of it. In a similar way, taking picnic blankets and seats outside may be all that is necessary to make the space work for a planned activity.

The changes you decide to make will, of course, depend on what activities you plan to take outside. Can you make permanent changes or will they have to be temporary ones? Check out who owns the land. Maybe you share the use of the land with others; so you will need to talk to them too.

Create a plan of your chosen space – the bigger the better, so it can be used as you develop your plans.

What do you want to do in your space?

The next stage is to think about the activities you might want to do outside. Look through the ideas in this book to inspire you. Talk with various groups and individuals within your church community, and also to other churches and groups to learn about what they have done. If you want to do lots of different things in one space, you will need to think about your priorities, the types of groups who might be interested in using the space and how you could develop your space so as not to restrict its uses.

Ask yourselves what you want to use your space for. Brainstorm ideas within your steering group or the wider church community. (See colour photo of brainstorming ideas on the website.)

Brainstorming ideas

Here are examples of what you might want to use a space for.

- To join together for worship – in small or larger groups.
- To sit for quiet contemplation and prayer – together or individually.
- A space to share your faith with the wider community.
- A place for remembrance.
- A community gathering space.
- A space for community activity, e.g. for community gardening, arts and crafts, or exercise.
- A space for uniformed organizations to meet and undertake activities such as camping and camp fires.
- A space for children and young people to meet and/or play.

- A space for wildlife.
- A shared space, for example with a nursery or playgroup, or a uniformed organization.
- A space for church events such as the summer fete, harvest festival or a dance.

Designing your space

For a permanent space

If you are designing a permanent space it would be good to create a vision statement that sums up what you want to do in your outside space. It shouldn't be too prescriptive, just something that illustrates what you are aiming for as you all work together. It could help you if you need to do some fundraising for your project. If you have a mission statement for your church, you will need to make sure it fits with that.

When creating a vision statement, start by brainstorming in small groups words and phrases that relate to how you want your space to be; this can be quite broad, and not too specific. Examples might be: inclusive, welcoming, prayerful, a space for the whole church to gather, colourful. Put these ideas together into a statement about your outdoor space, which could also contain elements of your church's mission statement.

It can be helpful to give your groups a starting point for their discussions, such as:

- Our outdoor space will be a place . . .
- We will use our outdoor space to . . .
- Our church will have an outdoor space that . . .

Take the best ideas and draw them together to create a vision statement you are all happy with.

You will need to organize your list of everyone's ideas into order of priority. Not everything may be achievable, or not all in one go. Group similar ideas together, as you may want to create a space where several different types of activity can occur. Write each idea on a sticky note, then prioritize them by creating a diamond pattern (see colour photo of priorities on the website) with your highest priority at the top, the lowest at the bottom and the majority in the middle.

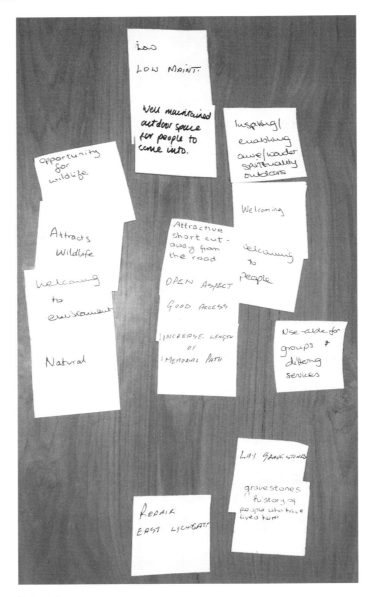

Priorities

Gather ideas for your open space: from other urban or rural public spaces, from the internet or books and magazines, from school sites or places used by churches or other faith communities such as monasteries or retreat centres. Collect images of places and spaces you like, but also of aspects of spaces you don't like, as that can be really helpful too.

A mood board of images might be useful. Display this alongside the proposed plan of your site. Some people may have used mood boards when planning home improvements, such as a new kitchen. The idea is to collect images of things you like and display them all in one place. These give you a feel of what you want to achieve; in a house situation it helps you, or a designer, create a room that both feels and functions in the way you want it to. A mood board for your outside space can be used in a similar way.

Begin by laying out your design on the ground where it is going to be located, so you create your design full-sized outside. You can use chairs to indicate where seating should go, flowerpots to show where you might have plants, or a rope to mark out a pathway. Use anything that can be moved around to develop your design. Take photos as you go along showing the different layouts. When you have made several different 'designs', ask people to comment on them before deciding on your final solution; don't expect your first attempt to be the best.

Depending on the scale and form of what you are planning to do, you may need to bring in a designer, or a specialist for a particular feature. For major changes intended to last for a long time, the expertise of a designer would be a worthwhile investment. They will pull all your ideas together and ensure your design works as a whole. The information you have gathered will help them come up with the best solution for your community, so the more preparation you do in advance, the more likely they will understand your vision.

While planning permission is unlikely to be necessary, do check with your planning department if you want to add new structures, especially if you are based in a conservation area or if your church is listed.

You may be able to call upon local talent – an artist to work with the community, or a gardening specialist to help create a growing area or to develop the planting in your space, or a wildlife expert to help you ensure that your place is great for animals and plants as well as humans. You may find that you have suitable people within your church or wider community, so try to use the skills and knowledge that are readily available to you.

Consider planning for use of the space at different times of day, or year. Do you need power for lighting or audio equipment, including musical instruments? How secure is the space? And one final, very important aspect is the question of who is going to maintain the site.

For a temporary space

Ask yourself questions related to your chosen activity. What do you want to be able to do in your space? Why are you deciding to use an outside space? What experiences do you want people to have? How long do you want it to last for? Who is going to use it? Could the space be used by more than one group within the church or wider community?

You may go straight to creating your changes if they are very temporary (see section below). You could do something slightly different each time you use the space, perhaps letting different people take the lead each time you hold an activity. It may lead to more permanent change in the end, once you have had a few test runs.

Making it happen

For a permanent space

Working on your project can really bring the community together, and this is particularly true when you are making it happen. Use the different skills and enthusiasms at your disposal. Getting people of all ages involved will help them to see the potential of the space and develop a real sense of ownership.

Be realistic about having lots of different people involved, however; remember that you may require a specialist for some elements. Make sure you have someone in charge of volunteers who knows what they are doing. Carry out a risk-benefit assessment (see the health and safety section). Check that you are insured both for undertaking the work and for using the space once it has been completed.

Jobs that the community could help with include clearing the site, painting, planting, creating sculptures, filling planting beds with soil and compost, moving features around the site. They can dig, shovel, build . . .

Don't forget these key features to consider:

- **Seating** – how many people are you creating a space for? What size are they (young children or adults, for example)? Do they need some shade from the sun? Is there shelter from wind and rain? Are people gathering to talk to each other or to listen to someone – the seating layout will depend on its use.
- **Storage** – having some secure storage outside can make it easier to use your space on a regular basis, and also help make the space more flexible in how it is used.
- **Security** – apart from secure storage, you may need to think about others' access to the site. Is entry to the site open or restricted? Will the materials you are using and features planned cope with different types of use, which might include unplanned visitors?
- **Health and safety** – make sure you undertake a risk-benefit assessment (see the section on health and safety) so that the changes you are making are safe.
- **Accessibility** – pathways, changes of level, height of seats, space for wheelchairs are all things you should be considering, along with visibility and sound around your space.
- **Make it special** – depending on the type of space and how long it is going to last you could include features such as planting, paintings, sculpture, wool bombing.

Storage shed

For a temporary space

An outside worship space or a quiet place for contemplation can be straight-forward to create and you will probably make the changes yourselves. Children will enjoy being involved, especially if the space is being changed for their use.

Use your imagination in the materials you use. Here are a few ideas to get you going:

- Logs or straw bales for seating. (See colour photo of temporary seating on the website.)
- A simple water feature.
- Candles.
- Lengths of bright cloth or sheets strewn overhead or around existing structures.
- A cross or icon.
- Flowers.
- Pictures or sculptures.
- A cairn (pile of pebbles).

Temporary seating

Celebrate!

Once you have achieved your goal and your outside space has been created, make sure everyone who has been involved has a chance to take part in a celebration. Also think how you can get the wider community participating. This is a great opportunity to appeal to others in a space that isn't a church building.

You could hold a service outside to bless the site and its future use, and those who have worked on it. If the site is not adjoining your church you could turn this into a procession or pilgrimage.

Make the most of your site being outside; focus on God's world around you in your celebrations. Also incorporate elements that you couldn't do inside. You could display banners that flutter in the wind, create a cairn (collect stones from different parts of the site and bring them together as part of your worship) or join together for a barbecue or picnic after a service.

Evaluate

Reviewing your changes periodically to see whether things have worked as you intended, or whether further changes are needed, is very useful. Most things can be improved upon or may be changed in the future, but don't forget to enjoy using the space you have created.

Ideas for being a wild church throughout the year

Children's activities

- Grow your own daffodils for Mothering Sunday by planting bulbs in the autumn. Note that daffodil bulbs are poisonous, so make sure they are labelled and left somewhere safe before planting.
- Can you support your uniformed organizations? They could perhaps camp in your outside space, or there may be features in your grounds that could be useful for them, e.g. seating, shelter, storage.

Church family activities

- Eating outside is a great way to bring the whole church family together, for example:
  - Picnics.
  - Bring and share meals.
  - Barbecues.
  - Meals cooked over a camp fire.
- Create a garden using plants mentioned in the Bible, or similar plants suitable for your location.

Men and boys

Many churches find that men are reluctant to take part in church activities. Outdoor-based activities could be a way to get them involved. However, there is no reason why other groups within the church couldn't do them too. Here are a few ideas that they might enjoy:

- Camping.
- Camp fires.

- Wilderness experiences/bushcraft activities.
- Building outdoor features, e.g. seating, allotments, shade sails.

Parents and toddlers

Churches often support new parents as part of their outreach work. Parents may well struggle with ideas for activities outside with their children. Children sit in front of screens for increasingly longer periods of time so it is more important than ever for children to have contact with the natural world. Here are some simple ideas for parents to use to help young children enjoy being outdoors:

- **Collecting colours** – cut out a strip of cardboard, about 10cm by 20cm, and stick a strip of double-sided sticky tape down the middle. Go outside and see how many different colours you can collect by finding things outside, then taking just a tiny piece of each object to stick on your card. For older children you can add a strip of paint chart next to the sticky tape to see if children can find a match for different colours. Make it harder by using different tones of one colour, such as green.
- **Den building** – children love dens and having a bag or box of resources such as sheets, blankets, ropes and clothes pegs will mean that there is always something to build with. A toy tea set or books to read will add to the fun.
- **Making shakers** – children love to make a noise as they sing. Use an old tin with a lid or a plastic bottle and collect from outside stones, bark or anything else that will rattle to put inside it. Secure the lid, perhaps with some tape, and you have an instant shaker. Go marching to their favourite songs and they'll love them even more.

Services

- Think about regularly taking services outside, all through the year. When planning your services always have this idea at the back of your mind and consider whether you can take all or part of your worship outside.
- You could decide at short notice to take the planned Sunday service outdoors, if the weather forecast is looking good. You will need to be aware of what this entails so you can quickly get ready without too long being spent in preparation to go outside.
- Why not burn your palm crosses outside as part of your Ash Wednesday service?

- On Palm Sunday, have a procession between two churches within your area as a sign of witness.
- Use the service ideas in this book to plan some of your worship outdoors.

Grow your own foliage for the flower arrangers

Even with only small grounds and gardens, think about what you could plant that would be useful for your flower arrangers throughout the year. Discuss with them what they would find useful – this might be not just flowers but also greenery.

Reaching out into the community

- Research different outdoor traditions for Christian festivals as they are celebrated around the world. Work with your local community to make them come alive in your area.
- For information on dementia-friendly design see Step Change Design: www. stepchange-design.co.uk; Thrive: www.thrive.org.uk; Sensory Trust: www. sensorytrust.org.uk; and the Alzheimer's Society: www.alzheimers.org.uk.
- Create areas where people can sit and find peace. Having seating in your grounds may encourage more people to use them. Consider your location and who might be encouraged onto your site; it will depend on your situation as to whether to have seating visible from outside your site or in a more secluded space.

Your church grounds and wildlife

Your church grounds can be a haven for wildlife. Areas that have been unbuilt on for centuries often have quite diverse areas of grass and other plants that are home to animals, birds and insects. However, creating an area for wildlife is not just about not maintaining it! In fact regular attention is required to ensure that habitats and sources of food are maintained. The following are a few habitats and food sources you can create and maintain in your church's grounds.

- Your boundaries can become sources of food or a habitat for wildlife. Planting native species to create a hedge can encourage wildlife to make a home in your grounds. Regular maintenance to your hedges should be undertaken during the winter or early spring, when birds and other animals are not nesting in them or feeding from their fruit; and avoid cutting back your hedges in the growing season.

- If you are looking to plant trees, consider using native species. Find out what grows well in your local countryside to help you choose what to plant in your area. Fruit trees are another idea. These can often be grown as cordons or espaliers, which don't take up very much room so they are excellent for planting in small spaces.

- The way you manage and maintain your grounds can have an impact on wildlife. Leaving discrete areas of grass at different lengths will ensure a variety of habitats and food sources for a wide range of wildlife. A large percentage of our native meadows have been lost within the last century, so encouraging wildflowers in your churchyard can have double the benefit of helping to retain a precious habitat along with looking lovely.

- In order to make your grounds still look neat and tidy, mow along the edges of the paths. Keeping grass short in these areas ensures that the grounds look cared for, and help to define the space.

- Gravestones and stone walls are often covered in lichens. They do not damage the stone and can actually protect them from erosion. So if possible leave them as they are.

- Put up bird or bat boxes in your grounds, or bird feeders or mini beast 'hotels'. A range of invertebrate and mammal houses are available, or you can make your own. Take advice from your local Wildlife Trust as to where to site such boxes and feeders. The Wildlife Trust should also be able to investigate the wildlife already living in your grounds and help you plan to make your area more wildlife friendly. In some places awards are given for the best churchyards for wildlife. The Living Churchyards and Cemeteries project is run by a number of trusts around the country. They provide detailed information on how to manage your grounds for wildlife.

Whatever you choose to do, whoever manages your grounds needs to know what you are trying to do. Create a simple management plan for your site, outlining the different habitats and how you intend to maintain the areas. Decide who will be responsible for undertaking the work, or divide your grounds into areas for various groups or individuals to look after. You may need to take it in turns to tend specific features that require more than the average maintenance.

Other sources of help and information

- While focusing on the outdoors, you should also think about how we care for creation. In England and Wales, Eco Church has resources and ideas for helping you to do this – they can be found at: www.ecochurch.arocha. org.uk. If you are based outside England and Wales, you may be able to take part in the Eco-Congregation programme, which can be found at: www. ecocongregation.org.
- Caring for God's Acre is a lottery-funded project supporting people caring for churchyards and burial grounds, found at: www.caringforgodsacre.org.uk.
- Churches can apply to a number of trusts for funding grounds projects. These are ever changing, so check through an online grant finder for what is currently available in your area.
- For further advice, help or training, or presentations on using or developing your own Wild Church, planning what you can do outside or making changes to your site, email Mary and Juno on: mejmidge@gmail.com, or follow us on Twitter: @wildchurchuk.